Guadalcanal 1942–43

C000091735

COMBAT

US Marine
VERSUS
Japanese Infantryman

Gordon L. Rottman

First published in Great Britain in 2014 by Osprey Publishing,
PO Box 883, Oxford, OX1 9PL, UK
PO Box 3985, New York, NY 10185-3985, USA
E-mail: info@ospreypublishing.com

Osprey Publishing is part of the Osprey Group

Print ISBN: 978 1 4728 0134 0
PDF ebook ISBN: 978 1 4728 0135 7
ePub ebook ISBN: 978 1 4728 0136 4

Index by Mark Swift
Typeset in Univers, Sabon and Adobe Garamond Pro
Maps by bounford.com
Originated by PDQ Media, Bungay, UK
Printed in China through Asia Pacific Offset Ltd

14 15 16 17 18   10 9 8 7 6 5 4 3 2 1

Osprey Publishing is supporting the Woodland Trust, the UK's leading
woodland conservation charity, by funding the dedication of trees.

www.ospreypublishing.com

Acknowledgments

The author appreciates Tom Laemlein of Armor Plate Press for his
photographic support. The US Marine Corps Historical Center was
especially helpful with much assistance provided by Charles Melson,
Chief Historian, and Kara Newcomer, Photo Historian. Much thanks
also goes to Akira "Taki" Takizawa for his input, and to Neil Grant and
the staff and trustees of the Small Arms School Corps museum and the
Imperial War Museum for providing photos of Japanese weaponry and
equipment.

Editor's note

US Marine battalions assigned to regiments are shown as, for example,
1st Battalion, 5th Marines as "1/5th Marines." The Japanese used Roman
numerals to designate battalions organic to regiments; such battalions are
shown as, for example, "II/124th Infantry." Japanese tank,
reconnaissance, engineer, shipping engineer, signal, and transport
"regiments" were actually of battalion size. Japanese names are shown in
the traditional Japanese manner with the surname or family name first,
followed by the personal name. Hyphens are used in Japanese officer
ranks, but not in American ranks. Some Japanese weapon designations
are shown in centimeters, following Japanese wartime practice. For ease
of comparison please refer to the following conversion table:

1 mile = 1.6km
1yd = 0.91m
1ft = 0.30m
1in = 2.54cm/25.4mm
1lb = 0.45kg

Comparative ranks

US Marine Corps	Imperial Japanese Army
Major General (MajGen)	Lieutenant-General (*Chūjo*)
Brigadier General (BrigGen)	Major-General (*Shōshū*)
Colonel (Col)	Colonel (*Taisa*)
Lieutenant Colonel (LtCol)	Lieutenant-Colonel (*Chūsa*)
Maj (Maj)	Major (*Shōsa*)
Captain (Capt)	Captain (*Tai-i*)
1st Lieutenant (1Lt)	Lieutenant (*Chū-i*)
2nd Lieutenant (2Lt)	2nd Lieutenant (*Shō-i*)
Chief Marine Gunner (CMG)	n/a
Marine Gunner (MG)	Warrant Officer (*Jun-i*)
Sergeant Major (SgtMaj)	Sergeant Major (*So-cho*)
Master Gunnery Sergeant (MGySgt)	n/a
Master Technical Sergeant (MTSgt)	n/a
First Sergeant (1stSgt)	n/a
Gunnery Sergeant (GySgt)	n/a
Technical Sergeant (TSgt)	n/a
Platoon Sergeant (PlSgt)	Sergeant (*Gun-so*)
Staff Sergeant (StfSgt)	Corporal (*Go-cho*)
Sergeant (Sgt)	Lance Corporal (*Hei-cho*)
Corporal (Corp)	Superior Private (*Joto-hei*)
Private 1st Class (PFC)	Private 1st Class (*Itto-hei*)
Private (Pvt)	Private 2nd Class (*Nito-hei*)

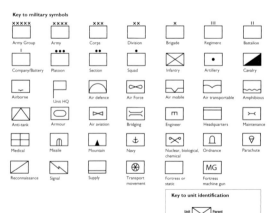

Key to military symbols

Army Group, Army, Corps, Division, Brigade, Regiment, Battalion, Company/Battery, Platoon, Section, Squad, Infantry, Artillery, Cavalry, Airborne, Unit HQ, Air defence, Air Force, Air mobile, Air transportable, Amphibious, Anti-tank, Armour, Air aviation, Bridging, Engineer, Headquarters, Maintenance, Medical, Missile, Mountain, Navy, Nuclear, biological, chemical, Ordnance, Parachute, Reconnaissance, Signal, Supply, Transport movement, Fortress or static, Fortress machine gun

Key to unit identification

Unit identifier, Parent unit, Commander, (+) with added elements, (−) less elements

CONTENTS

Introduction

At 0500hrs on August 7, 1942, 19,000 troops of the United States' 1st Marine Division (1st MarDiv) had their first sight of Guadalcanal to starboard. It was an island they had never heard of until the day before. They had known they were making a landing on a Japanese-held island, but were given no clue. They saw a dark craggy shape, a mysterious place stretching from horizon to horizon. Weather conditions had prevented Japanese reconnaissance-bombers from spotting the approach of Task Force 62 (TF 62). The Japanese knew a naval force had departed Hawaii, but were unaware of the main task force sortieing from New Zealand on July 22. The warning to Pacific outposts was not received on Guadalcanal until 0430hrs. An hour later the Japanese garrison on Tulagi Island across from Guadalcanal reported American ships in the channel. Surprise was complete. At 0613hrs the US Navy opened fire.

This amphibious landing was the start of the United States' first offensive land action – eight months after Pearl Harbor. The Japanese had established a naval base and three seaplane bases, and had built or were building 11 airfields throughout the Solomons, a double chain of islands running southeast to northwest separated by the New Georgia Sound – "The Slot" – with Guadalcanal the second-most southeastern island in the south chain.

The landing vehicle, tracked Mk 1 – LVT(1) – "Alligator" was not used as an assault vehicle at this time. They were put to good use hauling supplies from the beach to inland dumps and forward positions. While armed with a couple of machine guns, they were not armored and had a low belly clearance, causing them to belly out on stumps and deep mud. They were also used to move reserves to endangered sectors. They broke down at a high rate, being temperamental and having insufficient spare parts. As they broke down some were driven into rivers and used as supports for plank vehicle bridges. (USMC Historical Center)

Everything was at stake. It was a test of battle for Marines with no prior combat experience against battle-hardened Japanese soldiers, their fleets and air arms, and the operational and planning skills of their staffs. For both sides, distances were great, combat assets limited and hastily assembled, and logistical resources inadequate.

To the Marines aboard landing craft running toward a mysterious enemy-held island, however, the strategic implications of what was developing were of little importance. O-Hour on Beach Red, the code-name given to the landing area just to the east of Lunga Point on Guadalcanal, was set at 0910hrs. The landing craft used by Col LeRoy P. Hunt's 5th Marines commenced their 5,000yd run when they crossed the line of departure. They were expecting to be greeted by withering machine-gun fire and a *banzai* charge once they hit the beach. US intelligence had estimated a garrison of 5,000 construction and service troops plus a 2,100-man infantry regiment of the Imperial Japanese Army (IJA). At 0800hrs Marine detachments had landed on Tulagi Island to the north, and at 1200hrs Marines would come ashore on Gavutu and Tanambogo, farther to the east; on these islands, 900 Japanese troops would fight to the death against the 1st Raider and 1st Parachute battalions, 2/5th Marines, and 2/2nd Marines.

LtCol Frederick C. Biebush's 3/5th Marines on the left and LtCol William E. Maxwell's 1/5th Marines on the right swept onto shore as the naval gunfire was lifted from the 1,600yd-long beach. Not a shot met the Marines as they apprehensively moved across the narrow beach and through the rows of coconut palms devoid of underbrush. The Americans established a temporary defensive line along a backwater branch of the Tenaru River running parallel to the beach. The beachhead's flanks were defined by the Tenaru to the west and the Ilu River to the east. Col Clifton B. Cates' 1st Marines landed 20 minutes later and moved southwest toward Mount Austen, cautiously advancing only short distances and digging in for the night. There were no signs of the Japanese. Lunga Point was actually occupied only by 430 aviation service, Special Naval Landing Forces (SNLF, sometimes incorrectly called "Imperial Marines"), and guard force sailors of the Imperial Japanese Navy (IJN) plus 2,570 unarmed laborers, who fled without offering resistance.

The US advance was resumed on the morning of the 8th and the airfield was reached along with four abandoned Japanese camps. Japanese work had

A column of Marines take "ten." While cautious and in a strange land, the Marines landing on Guadalcanal were not overly anxious. They had trained at Guantánamo Bay, Cuba; Culebra Island, Puerto Rico; Virginia; North and South Carolina; and New Zealand. At one point they were scheduled for the North Africa invasion. They adapted quickly. Marines called the island "The Canal" or "Guadal"; the Japanese knew it as *Gadarukanaru* and assigned it the radio identification code RXN, but the island was known to soldiers fighting there as *Ga-Tō* (Hunger Island). Marines called it "Starvation Island." (USMC Historical Center)

Guadalcanal is 90 miles long and 30 miles wide, covering 2,047 square miles. It is mountainous, varying from 5,000ft to 7,600ft, and densely covered with lush jungle, although there were some clear acres just inland from the coast. On the north coast, where the action occurred, numerous streams and rivers flow out of the mountains across hilly coastal plains 3–10 miles wide. Beaches are narrow and there are few reefs. 22 miles northeast across The Slot are the Florida Islands with two initial Marine objectives, Tulagi (known as *Tsuragi* to the Japanese) and Gavutu islands, the district's former British administrative headquarters. Here a Marine battalion marches toward Henderson Field; a battalion could be moved from one end of the perimeter to the other in three hours. That included the time necessary for relieving units to take over the vacated positions and load out their equipment, crew-served weapons, and supplies. (USMC Historical Center)

progressed further on the airfield than the Americans had realized. Light resistance was encountered after crossing the Lunga River. The Japanese delivered their first air attacks from Bougainville. The US aircraft carriers lost a quarter of their fighters and were ordered to retire. During the early hours of August 9, the Japanese inflicted a severe pounding upon the Allied naval force off Savo Island and one Australian and three US cruisers were lost. That night the still partly loaded transports withdrew, leaving the Marines on their own; the Japanese mistakenly estimated only 7,000–8,000 Marines were on the islands. The Japanese high-speed supply, reinforcement, and shelling runs down The Slot, the "Tokyo Express," would soon commence – the Japanese called it Rat Transportation (*nezumi yusō*) as it ran at night. Based on Rabaul on the north end of New Britain, 600 miles north of Guadalcanal, and formed on May 18 with the specific mission of denying the Solomons to the enemy, the IJA's 17th Army (Lt-Gen Harukichi Hyakutake) would not land a force to drive off the 16,075 Americans until August 19.

The Solomon Islands, or *Soromon Shoto* to the Japanese, consist of seven major islands and almost 1,000 smaller ones. The arrival of TF 62 at this remote group of islands was the consequence of events beginning months before. Japanese forces launched from the Marshall Islands in the Japanese Mandate had occupied Rabaul in late January 1942. Most of the 500 Europeans in the Solomons evacuated after the Japanese bombed Tulagi, the district headquarters. With the Japanese preoccupied with securing the Netherlands East Indies, there were no Japanese incursions into the Solomons until mid-March when Buka, Bougainville, and Shortland were occupied at the north end. Naval and air bases there served as outguards for Rabaul and to support future Japanese offensives to the southeast. The battle of the Coral Sea (May 4–8, 1942) saw Japan's first major defeat and prompted the withdrawal of the Port Moresby, New Guinea invasion force. Corregidor fell to the Japanese at the same time. On May 4, SNLF units secured Tulagi and Gavutu, .Guadalcanal. Japanese seaplanes were to bomb Port Moresby from Tulagi. The Japanese were marshaling forces for the planned August invasions of New Caledonia, Fiji, and the Samoas, all defended by US troops. The battle of Midway (June 4–7, 1942) was disastrous for Japan and on July 11, the

New Caledonia, Fiji, and Samoa invasions were cancelled. However, the Japanese soon landed on New Guinea for an overland attempt at Port Moresby.

In mid-June the Japanese surveyed an airfield on Guadalcanal at Lunga Point (codenamed DIAL by the Americans) and began construction at the beginning of July. It was discovered by American aircraft on July 4. At the month's end it was bombed by the Americans to hamper construction. The United States had begun considering a move into the Solomons in March and planning began in May. The Operation *Watchtower* warning order was issued on June 26 with a tentative D-Day of August 1. It was soon postponed to August 7 owing to the time necessary to marshal and prepare the widely scattered US forces. Allied intelligence on the target area was scarce. Australian planters and British administrators from the area were consulted and coastwatcher reports were valuable. Existing navigation charts provided minimal data. There were no surveyed geographic maps. Aerial photographs provided the best data and sketch maps were made from these. Particularly good photos were taken by Boeing B-17 Flying Fortress missions on July 17 and August 2. The 1st MarDiv assistant operations officer, LtCol Merrill B. Twining, accompanied the latter mission and verified the landing beach appeared suitable. Aerial photos were up to date and showed stream and river locations and other features, but the vegetation hid land forms and provided no elevation data. Aerial photographs were taken when cloud cover permitted. The Japanese had even fewer maps and no aerial photographs. A sketch map prepared by the 5th Marines from data provided by an Australian caused difficulties. It misnamed some rivers and owing to the placement of place names, would lead to confusion about the location of Mount Austen, an initial objective.

Most of the fighting would occur in the vicinity of Lunga Point on the north-central coast. Lever Brothers coconut plantations covered the area and it was just inland that the Japanese began building their airfield, which would become Henderson Field. This area supported a modest road network with bridged streams. A coastal track ran from there to Koli Point 8 miles to the east and to Cape Esperance 30 miles away on the northwest end. The fighting would move westward from Lunga Point until the Japanese evacuated from Cape Esperance. That portion of the coastal plain was cross-compartmented by hills and ridges providing the Japanese defensible lines. The climate was hot and humid with frequent rain. Malaria, dengue fever, dysentery, and diarrhea decimated both sides. The first three months, the period covered in this study, saw both sides plagued with severe food, ammunition, and supplies shortages. The troops fighting on the island often felt they had been dumped there and forgotten.

Based on a map prepared by the 1st MarDiv D-2 (Intelligence) Section, this special task sketch map of the Lunga Point area on north-central Guadalcanal was used by the 5th Marines. The map's information was provided by a former island resident, an Australian. An arrow indicates the 5th Marines' planned route from Beach Red to the supposed location of "Mount Aesten" (actually Austen), the regiment's D-Day objective. However, the sketch clearly identifies the indicated feature as "Wooded Areas 'L' & 'TREE' Shaped on Grassy Knoll." "Mount Aesten" is written beneath the wording separated by a line and the mountain's approximate location is indicated by "X 1514". The names of the Ilu and Tenaru rivers have been inadvertently switched by the former resident. (USMC)

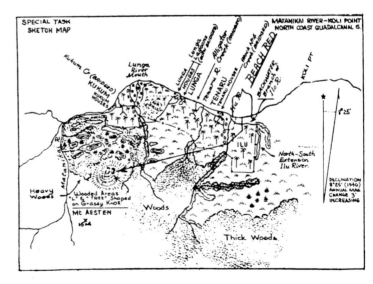

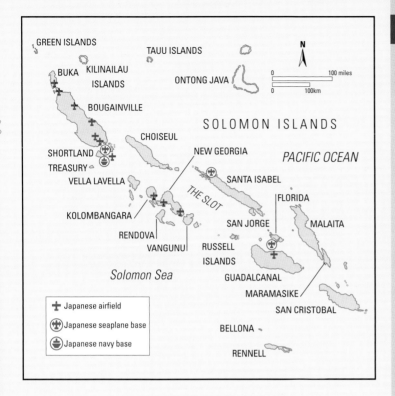

GREEN ISLANDS

TAUU ISLANDS

BUKA KILINAILAU ISLANDS

ONTONG JAVA

N

0   100 miles
0   100km

BOUGAINVILLE

SOLOMON ISLANDS

CHOISEUL

SHORTLAND
TREASURY

NEW GEORGIA

PACIFIC OCEAN

SANTA ISABEL

VELLA LAVELLA

THE SLOT

FLORIDA

KOLOMBANGARA

SAN JORGE

MALAITA

RENDOVA

VANGUNU

RUSSELL
ISLANDS

Solomon Sea

GUADALCANAL

MARAMASIKE

SAN CRISTOBAL

BELLONA

RENNELL

✚ Japanese airfield

✚ Japanese seaplane base

✚ Japanese navy base

9

Gurabasu

Aola

Indispensable Strait

The Guadalcanal campaign 1942–43

1   August 7, 1942: 1st MarDiv lands at Lunga Point, Guadalcanal.

2   August 19–21, 1942: The battle of the Tenaru.

3   September 8, 1942: Tasimboko Raid.

4   September 12–14, 1942: Henderson Field Attack and the battle for Edson's (Bloody) Ridge.

5   September 23–October 9, 1942: Three attacks to push the Marine western perimeter beyond the Matanikau River. The first US Army units arrive on Guadalcanal on October 13.

6   October 23–26, 1942: Matanikau Counteroffensive (battle for Henderson Field).

7   November 1–4, 1942: Point Cruz Offensive.

8   November 2–3, 1942: USMC forces mount the Koli Point Landing.

9   November 4, 1942: Carlson's Raiders land at Aola Bay.

10   November 5–December 4, 1942: Carlson's Raiders undertake their "Long Patrol."

11   December 15–31, 1942: The US Army carries out the Mount Austen offensive.

12   January 1–26, 1943: The US Army's Mount Austen offensive continues.

13   January 22–February 3, 1943: US forces clear the Point Cruz area.

14   February 1–8, 1943: The Japanese withdraw from Guadalcanal; on February 9, the island is declared secure by the Americans.

The Opposing Sides

ROLE, ORGANIZATION, AND TACTICS

If there were ever two opposing forces that could be described as military opposites, it was the US Marine Corps (USMC) and the Imperial Japanese Army (IJA). Virtually every aspect of the two organizations' roles and missions, motivation, organization, tactics, logistics, and command and control were different. What the two had in common was similarity of weapons – although these were employed differently – lack of preparedness for the brutal environment, and the dedication of the two forces' personnel. Tactics on Guadalcanal were kept simple, mainly because of the rough terrain with restricted visibility. The rugged terrain, dense vegetation, swamps, and weather hampered ground movement, be it by foot or scarce vehicles. Foot movement in the jungle was difficult day or night, especially by heavily loaded, exhausted troops. Native trails were few and not meant for heavy foot traffic. Vehicle-capable roads were even rarer. Some clearings were negotiable by vehicles and at low tide vehicles could drive on beaches. These were too exposed close to the front line for routine use.

USMC

Optimized for amphibious assaults, the 19,500-strong 1942 Marine division fielded three infantry regiments, an artillery regiment, special troops – HQ, special weapons (antitank and antiaircraft), parachute, light tank, engineer, and pioneer (shore party) battalions – and service troops. A Marine infantry regiment was similar to its Army counterpart and about the same strength: 3,168 compared to the Army's 3,200. The three infantry battalions were also similar and designed to close with and destroy the enemy in close combat on any terrain or climate. An infantry regiment was officially referred to as the 5th Marines, for example. The 1st MarDiv (MajGen Alexander A. Vandegrift)

deployed with its 1st and 5th Marines, and the 2nd MarDiv's attached 2nd Marines. Col Amor LeR. Sims' 7th Marines (1st MarDiv) would arrive from Samoa on September 18, 1942, and the 2nd MarDiv would relieve the 1st in January 1943. Its 6th and 8th Marines would also serve on Guadalcanal. The infantry regiment had a headquarters and service company, a weapons company, and three battalions. The battalions each had a headquarters (HQ) company, a weapons company – discussed below – and three rifle companies. The 1st Battalion included Companies A–D, the 2nd Battalion E–H, and the 3rd Battalion Company I plus K–M; Companies D, H, and M were weapons companies, and there was no Company J.

A Marine identified strongly with his company and the regiment was his tribe. The company CO ("Skipper") and first sergeant ("Top") provided a firm leadership team. The company HQ consisted of two officers and 27 enlisted including supply, cooks, and other support personnel. The three 42-man rifle platoons each consisted of a platoon commander (lieutenant), platoon sergeant (title and rank), platoon guide (sergeant), demolitions corporal, three messengers, and an attached Navy corpsman ("Doc") to provide immediate first aid and stabilize the wounded before they were evacuated. The rifle platoon's three nine-man rifle squads each had a squad leader (sergeant), assistant squad leader (corporal), an automatic rifleman and assistant, two scouts, and three riflemen, one doubling as a grenadier. All were armed with Springfield rifles except the automatic rifleman with an M1918A1 Browning Automatic Rifle (BAR) and the grenadier had a Mk III grenade launcher. Officially, the eight-man automatic rifle (AR) squad had a squad leader, two each of automatic riflemen and assistants, and three riflemen, but it appears many AR squads had three BARs. They were armed as a rifle squad, but the AR squad leader had a Reising submachine gun (SMG) for close-in protection. A few Thompson SMGs found their way into rifle platoons. All men were trained to operate all the platoon's weapons, with the exception of the grenade launcher, which was issued almost as an afterthought. The rifle company's 28-man weapons platoon had an HQ with the platoon commander, platoon sergeant, and two messengers. The 13-man machine-gun section had a section leader and two six-man squads, each with an M1919A4. The 11-man mortar section had two five-man squads each with a 60mm M2.

The battalion weapons company consisted of three HMG (heavy machine gun) platoons, each organized into two two-gun sections. Each gun was manned by a squad. This gave the company 12 HMGs plus 12 spares; it provided an HMG platoon to each rifle company and they were rotated between companies in the defense so they would be familiar with all companies. The heavy water-cooled guns were used in the defense phase, but after November when more mobile operations were conducted followed by the push to drive the Japanese west, the guns were less useful and it required much manpower to transport the guns, ammunition, and water cans over rugged terrain. Their long range and ability to maintain sustained fire was valuable when the riflemen assaulted hills and ridges, but often the dense forests hampered their ability to do so. In the next year's reorganization, the weapons company lost the spare HMGs. The mortar platoon had four 81mm M1 mortars; these proved to be an effective

While the M1917A1 water-cooled machine gun was excellent for static defensive fire support, when the men of the 1/1st Marines executed their counterattack on the Japanese left flank at the battle of the Tenaru, they made good use of the M1919A4 machine gun owing to its comparative light weight and the crew's ability to keep up with the rifle troops. The M1919A4 was fed by 250-round web belts with one red-tipped tracer to four ball rounds. The M1917A1 proved to be too heavy on the rugged terrain and its long range was unnecessary. (USMC Historical Center)

This USMC patrol demonstrates the wide intervals used when crossing semi-clear areas. The BAR man to the left has removed the weapon's bipod to save weight and one less thing to snag on dense vegetation. Palm plantations were usually devoid of underbrush, but this portion of a plantation is sprouting weeds and light brush. (USMC Historical Center)

weapon – the battalion commander's "artillery." The light HE (high explosive) shells could be fired very rapidly to break up infantry attacks with the heavy HE rounds (twice as heavy as the light) effective against bunkers. The AT platoon had four 37mm M3A1 guns and two .50-cal AA machine guns. The platoon was useful in the defense, but was not compatible to the infantry battalion's foot mobility. Owing to the negligible tank threat and 12 such guns in the regimental weapons company, this platoon would be deleted the following year.

The fighting in the Solomons would see many practical adjustments to the organization and role of the USMC infantryman. On Guadalcanal, the scouts were initially employed ahead of squads – "scouts out" – but it was discovered that if they were engaged at close range, they were often lost or cut off. Instead, they served as riflemen. The rifle squad's BAR was intended to provide covering fire as the riflemen maneuvered. In reality, owing to the limited visibility, the BAR advanced with the riflemen, often sweeping bursts of fire through the brush. The AR squad was meant to provide suppressive fire for the maneuvering squads, with the BARs alternating bursts so the BAR teams would not be changing magazines at the same time. In practice, vegetation denied the necessary fields of fire. As casualties and illness whittled away the rifle platoons the AR squad was absorbed into the rifle squads or became another maneuver squad; sometimes its BAR teams were loaned to rifle squads. Within two months a typical rifle platoon consisted of three 6–8-man squads, each led by a corporal or PFC (private first class). By the time the 1st and 5th Marines were relieved in December 1942, platoons fielded 12–18 men led by sergeants, corporals, or PFCs. A company might number 40–60 men. By the time the Marines were relieved, many crew-served weapons were served by two or three men.

Marine tactics were straightforward, involving a frontal attack if necessary or a flank attack if time, terrain, and enemy deployment allowed. Some successful Marine actions were battalion-sized attacks striking into the flank of enemy forces advancing to attack dug-in Marine positions. Initially, many Marine units were deployed on the beach to prevent a counterlanding. Companies on the perimeter would dispatch a platoon to beach defensive positions when coastwatchers reported Japanese ships running down The Slot. In the defense Marines made good use of the terrain, digging in along rivers, streams, and ridge lines. Little effort was made to protect exposed flanks other than outposts. The Japanese tended to conduct immediate frontal attacks once a Marine position was located. Two-man 3×3×6ft foxholes were dug. At this point there was little formal tactical training between infantrymen and tankers. At the time tanks were viewed as infantry-support weapons, but little training for close coordination between the tanks and infantry was undertaken. Owing to similar terrain and tactical conditions in the Northern Solomons, it would not be until the 1943 battle for Tarawa, essentially a large sandbar with little vegetation, that it was learned that tank–infantry training, coordination, and communication needed serious improvement.

IJA

The Japanese infantry division, varying in composition depending upon which organization it was under, was a general-purpose force intended for any conventional form of warfare on a wide range of terrain. A division's strength could range from 9,000 to almost 30,000 troops. Japanese divisions seldom fought as traditionally organized. They task-organized for each mission. They were typically named after their commander, Kawaguchi Detachment, for example, or they might be designated a "Force."

The infantry regiments fielded on Guadalcanal were basically the same, but there were minor organizational differences and allocation of weapons. The IJA infantry regiments fighting in the initial stage on Guadalcanal were: 4th, 16th, and 29th (2nd Division); 228th, 229th, and 230th (38th Division); and 124th (35th Infantry Brigade). The 28th Infantry Regiment (7th Division) also fought. Each regiment possessed an HQ plus signal, gun (six 7.5cm infantry guns), and antitank (six 3.7cm AT guns) companies. The three rifle battalions were designated I–III and typically fielded four rifle companies per battalion, numbered in sequence through the regiment (1st–12th). Each rifle battalion had a small HQ, battalion train, machine-gun company (eight or 12 HMGs), and gun company or platoon (four or two 7cm infantry guns). Some battalions had only three companies. Battalion machine-gun companies were designated, for example, 2nd Machine Gun Company, 4th Infantry.

Rifle companies had roughly 20 men in the HQ including the commander, personnel warrant officer, sergeant major (equating to first sergeant), supply and medical personnel, and eight messengers. The rifle company's three rifle platoons each consisted of a two-man HQ with the platoon commander (lieutenant) and liaison sergeant – this last was similar to a platoon sergeant, but mainly ensured orders were relayed via arm and hand signals and messengers. Each of the rifle platoon's three 13-man light-machine-gun (LMG) sections was led by a corporal and had a four-man LMG crew fielding three pistols or rifles and eight riflemen, one usually with a grenade launcher. Strengthened units had the addition of a two-man grenade-discharger crew in each section. Additionally, each rifle platoon had a discharger section with a leader, three two-man discharger crews, and six riflemen. Some units had rifle-company weapons platoons equipped with HMGs, but this was rare and believed not to have been used on Guadalcanal. The Japanese tended to control weapons more centrally than their American opponents.

With casualties, the rifle platoon's discharger section was usually absorbed into the LMG sections. The Japanese retained unit designations regardless of how small they shrunk. Regiments could dwindle to a few hundred men and battalions and companies remained intact even with a handful of men. This was not to instill a false sense of strength in undermanned units, but to retain the "soldier's family," his sense of belonging to a unit. No matter how much its strength dwindled, it was still the same cohesive unit. Most Japanese weapons were capable of relatively modest ranges. The jungle and hilly terrain

A Marine, wearing a Japanese camouflage cape, *tabi* split-toe black canvas shoes, and carrying a slung Arisaka rifle, demonstrates the techniques used by Japanese snipers to climb palms. In reality, most "snipers" – actually ordinary riflemen – were hidden on the ground. (Tom Laemlein/Armor Plate Press)

COMBAT | Rifleman, 2/1st Marines

On Guadalcanal the Marines went into combat for the first time wearing a gray-green uniform prone to fading and originally intended for fatigue duty – what the Marines called utilities. Previously they fought in khakis. This Marine carries minimal equipment, barely adequate for the environment, and an extremely reliable and high-quality rifle adopted 40 years earlier.

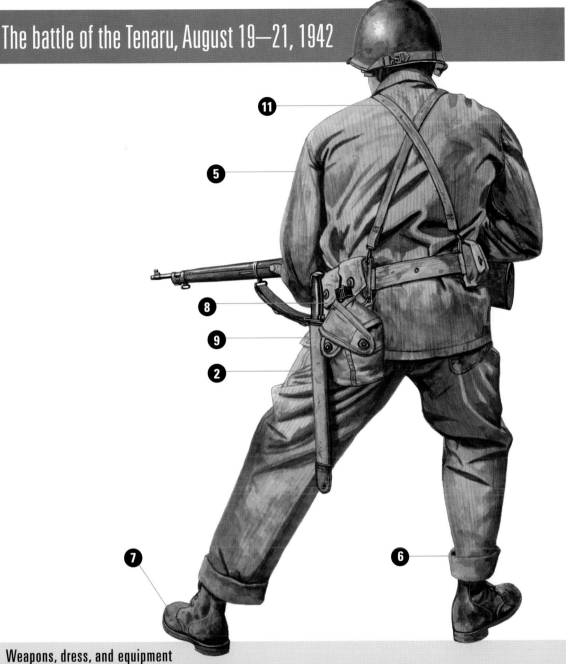

Weapons, dress, and equipment

The World War I Springfield .30-cal M1903 rifle (**1**) still armed the Fleet Marine Force. The semi-automatic Garand M1 rifle would not fully arm the FMF until late 1943. The Springfield "oh-three" was bolt-action with a five-round magazine. He carries a 16in-blade M1905 bayonet in an M1910 scabbard (**2**). Riflemen carried up to four yellow-painted Mk II "frag" grenades (**3**) – painted olive drab from 1943 as the enemy could find them in the dark to throw them back.

The OD M1 steel helmet (**4**) or "steel pot" was worn with a resin-impregnated fiber liner to improve ballistic protection. Camouflage covers were not worn at this time. The utility coat (**5**) at the time had a single small chest pocket and two larger skirt pockets. The herringbone cotton utilities faded quickly with weathering and washing. The utility trousers (**6**) were worn with the cuffs turned up for ventilation, while the hot, chafing, circulation-restricting, water-retaining, lace-up leggings were universally discarded. Most went without underwear as it retained sweat to cause rashes – "jungle rot." Ankle-high service shoes (**7**) or "boondockers" were often double-soled and worn with or without tan socks.

Web or "782" gear (named after the issue form) consisted of the ten-pocket cartridge belt (**8**) holding 20 five-round loading clips, 1-quart canteen with a cup nested in the canteen carrier (**9**), first-aid pouch (**10**) with field dressing and sulfa powder packets, and M1941 two-piece suspenders (**11**), to which the haversack was attached when carried.

Two Arisaka shoulder arms, the upper being the 6.5mm Meiji Type 38 (1905) short rifle and the 7.7mm Type 99 (1939) rifle. The Type 38 long rifle was of the same length as the Type 99; both were used by the infantry, while the Type 38 short rifle was used by engineers and artillerymen. The bayonet is the 15½in Meiji Type 30 (1897) (*juken*) issued to all personnel whether they had a rifle or not. (Neil Grant)

made short ranges a moot point. In the defense the Japanese sited weapons to engage at close ranges, in effect ambushing the advancing enemy at close, even point-blank ranges. Defenses were often designed to allow the enemy to enter the defense zone unknowingly. The defenders would open fire not only at close ranges, but from the flanks and even the rear from different directions.

In terms of Japanese tactics, the terms "defense," "retreat," and "surrender" were omitted from manuals as they were deemed to be detrimental to morale and the military spirit. The rule was to attack at unexpected times and points, along unanticipated routes and often with unfavorable force ratios to increase the surprise factor. The Japanese would make every effort to attack the flanks or to envelop the enemy from both flanks and cut him off from his support. This was attempted on several occasions on Guadalcanal. The Japanese frequently attacked frontally, always with disastrous results. Contrary to perception, the Japanese had no jungle-warfare training. There was no place to undertake it. The 38th Division had fought only in China and Hong Kong. The 2nd Division had seen combat on Java and the Philippines and the 35th Infantry Brigade in Singapore and Borneo, giving them some jungle experience, but most of the actions in those places were road-bound. Regardless, it was more than the Marines possessed. The Japanese were more experienced at night operations. They conducted probes to locate defenses to cause the enemy to fire and reveal his positions. They also made extensive use of "snipers," to warn of and slow the advancing enemy. The "snipers" were regular riflemen lacking specialized training and telescopes.

The Japanese did not always practice their doctrine, often violating basic fundamentals. Their biggest flaw was an unrealistic underestimation of the enemy. This stemmed from a combination of overconfidence, arrogance, and over-reliance on the strength of spirit. The result was an expectation that the enemy would do as Japanese plans had estimated while the Japanese themselves were often too inflexible to adapt to unanticipated enemy actions and reactions. The Japanese were deficient in combined-arms training. Combined infantry and artillery support were usually adequate, but once action commenced the artillery tended to stay with the agreed-upon fire plan and were unresponsive to changes. If they did change the plan it was often too late. This was often due to poor communications and branch competiveness between the artillery and infantry, the former considering the infantry a second-class branch.

FIREPOWER

For the most part, early in the war Japanese arms were of high quality in regards to manufacture. Some possessed design flaws and were overly complex, especially machine guns. American weapons, designed for European-style warfare, were of high quality, but there were exceptions such as the Reising SMG. The Japanese focused on warfare in China and Manchuria with cold climates and broad, open expanses. However, many of their weapons were relatively short-ranged. This of course proved irrelevant in jungles and the Japanese developed tactics to capitalize upon this. The restricted visibility imposed by vegetation and darkness and extremely short ranges required high volumes of automatic fire. All in all, regardless of differences between both sides' weapons, if they had exchanged weapons, the outcome would have been no different. For comparison, a 1,100-man, four-company IJA battalion had 37 LMGs, 36 5cm grenade dischargers, 12 HMGs, and two 7cm infantry guns. A 933-man three-company USMC battalion had 54 BARs (comparable to Japanese LMGs), six LMGs, 12 HMGs (plus 12 spares), two .50-cal MGs, six 60mm mortars, four 81mm mortars, and four 37mm AT guns.

USMC

The Marine Corps took "every man a rifleman" seriously. The Springfield .30-cal M1903 rifle was rugged, reliable, accurate, and considered the pinnacle of military bolt-action rifles. Loaded with a five-round charging clip, the 43.2in-long, 8lb 11oz M1903 could be used to maintain a rate of 10–15 aimed shots a minute, up to 20rds/min. The Marines had adopted the semi-automatic Garand M1 rifle in 1940, but production priority went to the Army. The Fleet Marine Force was not entirely armed with the M1 until late 1943. The Marines of Guadalcanal did not see it until the Army arrived. The Marines trained at known distance ranges ("KD range") with targets set at 200, 300, and 500yd. They were allotted 300 rounds for practice and qualification firing. They fired from prone, sitting, kneeling, and standing positions. For some targets they were required to change from one position to another between shots. While teaching good marksman skills for a conventional battlefield, it did little to prepare them for quick, short-range engagements with fleeting targets that shot back.

Thompson .45-cal M1928A1 SMGs with 20-round magazines and some 50-round drums saw use. The Marines had adopted the .30-cal M1 carbine, but these were not available during the fighting on Guadalcanal. Individuals assigned the weapon were armed instead with Springfields or .45-cal M50 Reising SMGs with 20-round magazines. SMGs were good for

Marines cleaned their weapons daily owing to rain, mud, and dust. The leftmost man holds a Reising M55 submachine gun with a wire folding stock usually issued to paratroopers. The man second from left holds a more common Reising M50 with a fixed wooden stock. Manufactured with poor tolerances and lower-grade metal, the Reising was prone to jamming and rusting, leading to it being called the "Rusting gun," and reputed not even to make a good club. The seated man second from right works on his M1918A1 BAR. (Tom Laemlein/Armor Plate Press)

The business end of a .30-cal M1917A1 machine gun occupies a hastily dug emplacement. Crews would habitually carry two to three empty sandbags. The 250-round ammunition box is a wooden M1917A1, which was being replaced by the M1 metal box. (Tom Laemlein/Armor Plate Press)

OPPOSITE

The Nambu 6.5mm Type 96 (1936) LMG seen here was used alongside the similar Nambu Type 99 (1939) LMG, but not in the same units. The Type 99 differed visually in that it had a cone-shaped flash hider, a monopod on the butt, and had a larger barrel locking catch. The standard bayonet could be fitted on either weapon. (Neil Grant)

spraying underbrush, but offered limited penetration. The Mk II fragmentation hand grenade, AKA "frag" or "pineapple," was a powerful grenade. They were reliable and the delay time accurate. Another grenade was the Mk III concussion, AKA "demolition" or "demo" grenade. Grenades were useful at night because they would not reveal Marine positions, could be thrown into dense vegetation where the enemy was hidden, and were effective for knocking out pillboxes. US grenades were much more powerful than Japanese grenades. The early fuses made a pop when ignited, thereby alerting the enemy. AN-M8 white smoke grenades were available for screening. Little known is the French-designed World War I Mk III Vivien-Bessières (VB) rifle grenade launcher. It threw a 50mm Mk I grenade to 180yd, longer-ranged than the Japanese rifle grenade launcher. The .30-cal M1918A1 BAR was key. This pre-war version was capable of semi-and full-automatic fire (the M1918A2 fired at low and high full-automatic rates only). Rather than having the bipod mounted at the muzzle, it was situated forward of the handguard, but was often removed to reduce weight. The BAR ran through a 20-round magazine rapidly, making it less than ideal for suppressive fire.

USMC rifle company support weapons included the 60mm M2 mortar, with a 1,965yd range and a maximum of 30–35rds/min (sustained rate of 18rds/min), and the air-cooled, tripod-mounted Browning .30-cal M1919A4 LMG. At battalion level was the Browning .30-cal M1917A1 HMG, a water-cooled gun mounted on a heavy stable tripod and intended for long-range sustained supporting fire. The weapons could be attached down to platoon level, but the 60mm mortars remained under company control and the 81mm mortars under battalion control. Platoon leaders became adept at siting and controlling the attached weapons. The Japanese tended to keep crew-served weapons under the control of the echelon they were assigned to, i.e., HMGs stayed under battalion control rather than being attached to rifle companies, especially in the attack. In the defense they might be attached to companies. After the battle of the Tenaru, preparations were made to improve the American defense to include coordinating for Marine aircraft to fly close-support missions. This was seriously hampered by the lack of suitable air–ground radios and because ground panels marking Marine positions could not be seen at night. Artillery coordination was adequate, but relied on telephones, and cut wires were a problem. More radios would have been invaluable.

IJA

The basic weapons around which IJA tactics evolved were the rifle, bayonet, hand grenade, grenade discharger, and LMG. Japanese platoon tactics were so focused on the LMG that what would be called a rifle squad in other armies was called a LMG section (squad). Riflemen were intended to protect the LMGs, while LMGs protected HMGs. Most infantrymen were trained to operate all of a platoon's weapons, but cross-training was minimal, especially with the grenade dischargers, and there was an apparent lack of motivation or confidence in taking over other weapons. Arisaka rifles were well made, reliable, and rugged, but heavy and awkward for small-statured Japanese. Their long barrels reduced muzzle flash, but easily snagged on vegetation; especially since the Japanese habitually fixed bayonets in combat. The 6.5mm Meiji Type 38 (1905) was the most widely used, at least in the early stages. The 7.7mm Type 99 (1939) was present, but initially in fewer numbers. Both were loaded by five-round charging clips. The advantage of the 7.7mm over the 6.5mm was the former's ability to penetrate vegetation and foxhole parapets. The 7.7mm round was ballistically similar to that used by the Springfield. The 6.5mm was the smallest and least powerful of the many 6.5mm rounds in use worldwide and no 6.5mm tracers were available.

Japanese grenades generated little blast and poor fragmentation. That is not to say they did not inflict casualties. They had an erratic delay time and frequently failed to detonate. The fuses made an audible "pop" when ignited. Americans were taught to advance upon hearing the pop to avoid the blast as the Japanese ducked for cover. They also smoked for three seconds before detonating with a hissing sound, allowing Americans to discover and throw them back. The Type 97 (1937) grenade arming pin was pulled and the percussion cap struck on a solid object – helmet, rifle stock, boot heel, tree, etc. – to activate the 4.5-second fuse, giving advance warning to the enemy. The Type 91 (1931) was similar in design, but could be fired from the spigot-rifle grenade launcher with the same designation and would fit on both 6.5mm and 7.7mm rifles. It could also be fired from the 5cm grenade discharger. A small propellant charge was screwed into the bottom for discharger firing. For rifle launching a finned tailboom was screwed in and launched by a wooden-bulleted cartridge. It had an 8–9-second delay to allow

ABOVE
The Type 97 (1937) fragmentation hand grenade (*shuryudan*) was one of the most widely used Japanese grenades. There was a threaded well in the base for the grenade discharger propellant charge. To operate the arming pin was pulled, the safety cover pulled off, the percussion cap struck on a solid object, and thrown. This grenade is held in a rare grenade belt carrier. (© IWM MUN 4655)

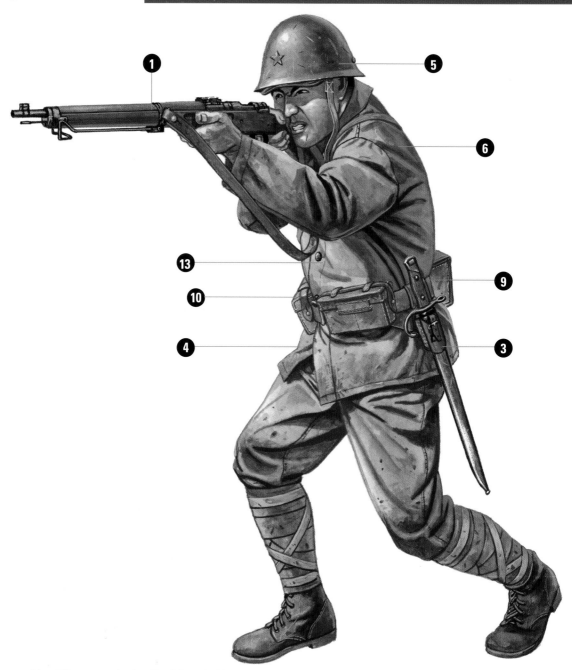

Most IJA troops arrived on Guadalcanal with greenish-tan to olive-drab cotton summer uniforms. Few units had the similar tropical uniform, with underarm ventilation and in a dark green color that blended better into the jungle. Equipment was simple, but well made at this time. Both 6.5mm Type 38 (1905) and 7.7mm Type 99 (1939) rifles were issued depending on the unit and where it was previously stationed.

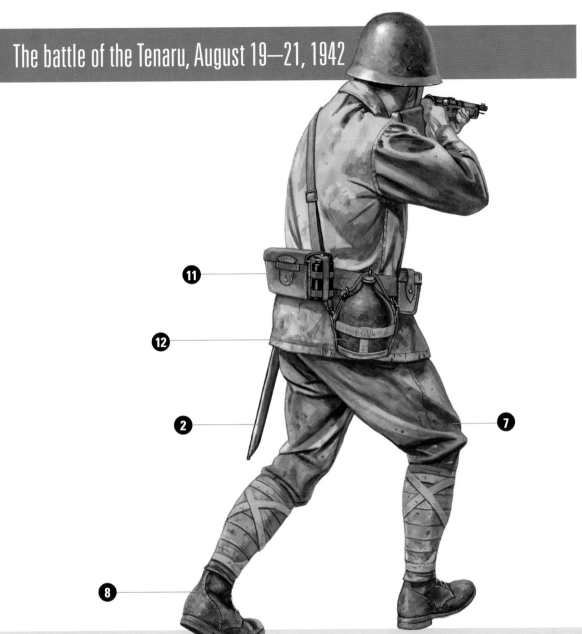

Weapons, dress, and equipment

The Arisaka 7.7mm Type 99 (1939) rifle (**1**) armed most units deployed from Japan, China, and Manchuria, but many still had the 6.5mm rifle. The heavy rifle was bolt-action with a five-round magazine. The Meiji Type 30 (1897) bayonet (**2**) had a 15½in blade. The hooked bayonet guard was intended to hook and yank an opponent's bayonet and even disarm him. In the jungle the bayonet was just something else to snag on vegetation since it was habitually carried attached to the rifle in combat. The steel scabbard was attached to a leather belt frog (**3**). Most soldiers carried in their pockets at least two Type 97 (1937) fragmentation hand grenades (**4**), which proved weak and unreliable, the fuse being affected by the humidity.

The Type 92 (1932) steel helmet (**5**) offered little real protection and was later often discarded. The field cap was commonly worn under the helmet. The Type 98 (1938) summer tunic (**6**) had breast

and skirt pockets while the Type 5 (1930), still in wide use, had only breast pockets. The trousers (**7**) could be three-quarter or full-length. The light cotton fabric did not hold up well in the tropics. Type 5 (1930) marching shoes (**8**) were made of horsehide and soon fell apart resulting in the wide wear of sandals or even going barefoot.

Meiji Type 30 (1897) personal equipment was mostly leather and held up poorly in the tropics – later rubberized canvas was used – and consisted of a one-size-fits-all service belt (**9**), two cartridge boxes (**10**) each holding 30 rounds, a reserve cartridge box (**11**) holding 60 rounds with an oil container on the right end, and Type 94 (1934) 2½-pint canteen (**12**) with web sling. The leather gear deteriorated in the tropics and rubber-treated equipment was later issued. A field dressing and triangular bandage (**13**) were carried in a left inside tunic pocket.

airbursts when fired from the grenade launcher and grenade discharger. To launch from those weapons the aiming pin was pulled and the grenade fired, the recoil activating the percussion fuse.

The 5cm Type 89 (1929) heavy grenade discharger ("knee mortar") could fire hand grenades with propellant charges, pre-rifled mortar rounds, and pyrotechnic signals. It had a 650m (710yd) range with mortar rounds and 200m (218yd) with grenades. It was mainly used for close-in fires. The squad's LMG was its base of fire, covering maneuvering riflemen. The Nambu 6.5mm Type 96 (1936) and 7.7mm Type 99 (1939) LMGs were similar and of course issued on the basis of the caliber of the rifles issued to the squad. Both were bipod-mounted, had a top-feed 30-round magazine, quick-change barrel, and could be fitted with a 2.5× telescope. They could be fitted with a bayonet, emphasizing the Japanese inclination for close combat regardless of the weapons' weight. They fired full-automatic only, but individual shots could be squeezed off. Marines called them "woodpeckers" because of their sound. An advantage they had over the Marine's BAR was ten additional rounds in a magazine that was faster to change, allowing the Nambu to provide better sustained fire. They were also 1½lb and 4½lb heavier than a BAR, respectively. At battalion level was the Nambu Type 92 (1932) HMG. This tripod-mounted gun was fed by 30-round feed strips. It used a semi-rimmed 7.7mm round, different than the rimless 7.7mm used in rifles and LMGs. The Type 92 could fire the rimless, but was prone to jamming.

LEADERSHIP AND COMMUNICATIONS

Command and control of a small unit is a challenge for even the best of leaders, but the environment and circumstances on Guadalcanal were particularly difficult for both sides. The rugged terrain and dense vegetation made observation and control hard, and more so because so much night action occurred. Besides swamps, mud, gullies, and streams, the vegetation limited visibility to the extent that nearby landmarks could not be seen. The often overcast sky turned it pitch black. Even with clear skies and moon and starlight, the overhead canopy created complete darkness. Battlefield communications, regardless of recent technological advances, were no better at this stage of the war than in World War I. Radios were in wide use, but below battalion level, they didn't exist. Field telephones and messengers were the main means of communications.

USMC

Placing all four squads on line in the jungle created too wide a span of control. Squad leaders had to be relied on to do the right thing as they were not always in sight of the platoon leader. Often one squad was held back protecting a flank and this reduced the span of control. Patrols were critical to locate the enemy and determine where he was massing. USMC patrols varied from half-squad to company strength depending on the mission and opposition. Small reconnaissance patrols avoided contact, but larger patrols would engage if discovered. Squads rotated patrol duty and a man could expect three or four a week. Since maps were non-existent, reconnaissance was essential to locate obstacles, determine routes, and identify landmarks, much less to locate the enemy. Marine NCOs were selected on the basics of proficiency, knowledge of weapons and tactics, bearing, and reliability, but most of all, their leadership ability. There were no NCO schools other than a few hours set aside here and there by the first sergeant. Natural leadership abilities were essential, and this included gaining the men's respect. Even when the sergeants and corporals became casualties, the most capable men were selected, and only rarely were promoted when taking over their duties. For the most part the other PFCs and privates accepted that a man of their rank was now in charge.

There were two messengers in the rifle company's HQ, three in each of the rifle platoons, and one in the weapons platoon. The rifle platoons detached one messenger to company HQ. The messengers were employed in any manner necessary to relay orders and requests (ammunition, for example) – that is, dispatched from platoons to their subordinate squads or to the company HQ. MCT-1 alert telephones allowed the companies and battalion to maintain contact. Sometimes an outpost or platoon somewhat remote from the main company position would also receive a telephone. Patrols, moving a short distance, sometimes carried a telephone to report back information, request fire support or reinforcement. It was awkward, but allowed real-time communications instead of messengers or waiting until they returned to report. No mention is made of the Marines using pyrotechnic signals. The later colored smoke grenades had not yet been adopted. Some use was made of semaphore flags by units operating along the coast for signaling to landing craft and fire-support destroyers. The Marines had 27 prescribed arm and hand signals for silent communications within platoons. They also created their own unofficial signals – two knuckle-raps on a rifle stock meant to fall back if the enemy was spotted on patrol. Jungle visibility limited these signals' use, even in daylight. It was essential for troops to stay alert for signals, often relayed from man to man in vegetation, and to respond to it immediately. If no signals were seen, troops followed the example of what nearby troops were doing.

Two signalmen man a battalion message center with Army EE-8 field telephones. They also used MCT-1 alert telephones (MCT = Marine Corps Telephone). Telephones were the main links between companies, battalions, and regiment. Allied codenames included ARTHRITIS for the Solomon Islands, BEVY for Guadalcanal, and CACTUS for the Guadalcanal–Tulagi objective area for Operation *Watchtower*. The Marines called it "Operation *Shoestring*" as it was quickly launched with inadequate support and logistics. The radio callsign was RXN. Note the burlap and woven rice straw bags used as sandbags. Many types of Japanese bulk rations were packed in such bags and the Japanese themselves routinely used them as sandbags. (Tom Laemlein/Armor Plate Press)

IJA

Japanese officers had been indoctrinated to believe that any enemy of the Empire was inferior with respect to military doctrine, military spirit, and dedication to the cause. This was driven in to the point that it was fully accepted that the superior Japanese would prevail. As such, when the enemy deployed in an unexpected manner or possessed unexpected capabilities – be it spirit, weapons, tactics, etc. – the Japanese were unable to react effectively. The matter was aggravated by poor, unresponsive communications and limited logistical capabilities. Officer cadets were selected through a series of rigid examinations. In theory this process was open to all classes, but families had to pay the

Heavy at 12lb, the Type 92 (1932) was the principal Japanese field telephone. Besides voice communications it had a buzzer and code key. Captured phones could be used in Marine wire circuits. The Japanese used a ground return system requiring only a single-strand wire and a spike driven into the ground and connected to the phone, while the Marines used two-strand wire, which entailed more weight. (© IWM COM 185)

considerable ration bill for three years in cadet school and this excluded the lower classes. In spite of the entrenched class system and the wide chasm between other ranks and officers, officers were expected to be as tactically and technically proficient as their men. They also willingly shared the sufferings and privations of combat and in many cases were tougher than their charges. Japanese NCOs were selected from the roughest, most stern recruits after three months' training. Their level of practical experience was often limited, but their authority was boundless. Rather than serve as examples, to instruct, guide, and look over, Japanese NCOs were more like foremen. They taught by repetition and disciplined by instantaneous physical punishment. Regardless of the *Five Principles of Battle Ethics* – loyalty, courtesy, courage, truthfulness, and frugality – the treatment of other ranks by NCOs differed drastically from the American model. Every mistake, every omission, and lack of vigilance and attention to detail were swiftly and harshly dealt with. Beatings were frequent and routine, not only in training, but in assigned units. The soldiers' fear of repercussion for mistakes and even the appearance of usurping authority often stifled initiative. It was for this reason that troops – including NCOs and junior officers – often failed to exploit tactical situations or even, for example, took over a weapon whose gunner was killed. They had not received permission to do so and feared the consequences.

The rifle company's HQ was assigned eight messengers. One would be detailed to each platoon. Those remaining at the HQ would carry messages to platoons and the battalion if telephone lines were not laid. This often occurred in the attack. Lines would be laid to the company assault position and messengers from the advancing companies would report back so information and requests could be telephoned to the battalion. This system often broke down in a night-time action. The Japanese used 35mm Taisho Type 10 (1921) flare pistols with at least a dozen different freefalling and parachute-suspended colored flares. There were also a variety of colored flare and smoke rounds for the 5cm grenade discharger. Sometime numerous multiple colored flares were fired at night from different locations before an attack to "confuse" the Marines. Within platoons, riflemen were used as messengers under the control of the liaison sergeant. The Japanese had no officially prescribed arm and hand signals – units developed their own. They also tapped on wood, whistled like birds, waved their arms, or shouted. Outposts and snipers communicated by jerking wires strung between their posts.

LOGISTICS AND MORALE

While air battles were common along with Japanese bombing raids, air transport contributed little. Instead, both sides relied on sea transport to reach the area of operations, resupply the troops, and move them within the area of operations. For landing troops and supplies, ship-to-shore movement, and intra-area repositioning, coastal freighters, barges, and landing craft were employed. Destroyers were used as high-speed transports. The United States and Japan were sea powers, but the United States commenced the campaign with limited resources, which were initially denied ready access to the area owing to Japanese sea and air capabilities from nearby bases. The Japanese established a series of hidden barge staging bases on islands from Bougainville to Guadalcanal – over 330 miles. The south end of Bougainville and nearby Shortland Island were the main Japanese bases. The main American bases supporting Guadalcanal were considerably farther away; Nouméa was more than 1,000 miles away, with Espíritu Santo over 650 miles distant. American sea forces were hampered by greater distances from their bases. Critical to the campaign were shallow-draft landing craft with drop bow ramps, supplemented by other small craft ranging from barges to ships' long boats. Most small craft movements occurred at night to avoid aircraft.

With respect to morale, the battle for Guadalcanal pitted two divergent military systems against one another. Doctrine, tactics, weapons, and equipment were obviously different, but the greatest difference was a more intangible factor, military *esprit de corps*. A Japanese soldier and a US Marine were truly warriors.

USMC

The 1st MarDiv was delivered to Guadalcanal aboard 19 transports and four destroyer-transports. With the decision to mount the operation and depart on July 22, only 11 days were allotted to unload and reload at Wellington, New Zealand. Constant rain resulted in the disintegration of cardboard boxes and paper sacks containing commercially packed rations. The plan allowed only two days to unload the ships' load, 60 days' supply and ten units of fire – an arbitrary number of rounds based on average daily expenditure in heavy combat, not a weapon's basic load – before the carriers and surface combatants withdrew. When the ships withdrew to Nouméa on August 9, they left the Marines with four units of fire and 37 days' rations. Captured Japanese food added 14 days' rations. Only two daily meals were provided.

In 1942 there were few ramped landing craft available to the Americans capable of delivering vehicles and artillery. Here a 1-ton cargo truck, mounting a .50-cal M2 machine gun, drives onto Beach Red from a 45ft landing craft, mechanized Mk 2 – LCM(2). This particular "Mike boat" belonged to the troop transport USS *President Jackson* (AP-37). (USMC Historical Center)

Most of the 1st MarDiv's jeeps and 1-ton trucks were loaded, but only 25 percent of the 2½-ton trucks. The number was reduced because higher staffs wrongly assumed the trucks would be mostly unusable on the island, but also to provide shipping space for 130 LVT-1 Alligator amphibian tractors ("amtracs"). In all, the division deployed with fewer than half its vehicles. At night the trucks were assembled to transport reserves to endangered sectors. The Marines used 35 operational Japanese trucks, but they proved flimsy and as they broke down, were cannibalized.

Wet and muddy Marines unload a landing craft during their advance. Landing craft would periodically resupply troops advancing along the coast and evacuate casualties and the ill. The military policemen standing to the left served as a "traffic controller." Eight landing craft were left behind in a boat pool when TF 62 departed and were valuable for delivering patrols, resupplying units advancing along the coast, and transferring troops between Guadalcanal and the Florida Islands. These included LCM(2) (landing craft, mechanized Mk 2); LCP(L) (landing craft, personnel (large)); and LCP(R) (landing craft, personnel (ramp)). (Tom Laemlein/Armor Plate Press)

American engineer equipment was not unloaded, leaving the engineers only Japanese equipment – six road-rollers, two narrow-gauge trains with hopper cars, and 50 handcarts. The engineers focused on completing Henderson Field and later started a fighter strip. They maintained and extended the coastal road and the beachhead road network. The streams had been bridged by the British and all had been seized intact by the Americans. As the Marine perimeter was pushed westward, jeep trails followed so supplies could be delivered by vehicles. Streams and gullies were bridged by timber or fuel-drum floating bridges. By mid-October 1942 the besieged Marines had received more aircraft, fuel, aerial ordnance, construction troops, and maintenance crews, but the perimeter defenders were still short of ammunition and rations. The troops were exhausted and suffering from malaria, dysentery, and other illnesses – "dizzying fever and nausea." Diarrhea was serious and spread by masses of flies rising from rotting bodies and open latrines. October 13, however, would be a landmark day for the ragged defenders of the American perimeter. Early that morning two transports arrived and unloaded the first US Army troops to reach the island, the Americal Division's 164th Infantry Regiment.

For the Marines, belief in the Corps was a primary motivation, if not *the* motivation; that and their loyalty to their squad and platoon. Some veterans characterized their compulsory dedication to the Corps as brainwashing, but few bore regrets. All were volunteers. Cohesion, a sense of belonging to a unit, was essential. Regardless of the patriotic movies and articles of the time, they did not fight for America, the flag, democracy, Mom, apple pie, or even the Corps, they fought for one another, for their comrades. American morale would prove resilient in the face of near-constant attacks. Following the battle of the Tenaru the Japanese focused their efforts on Henderson Field, with noontime bomber raids from Rabaul joining the Tokyo Express's frequent bombardments, nocturnal nuisance bombings and flare drops, and attacks from Japanese stragglers in the jungle. While the primary target was the airfield, stray bombs, falling AA shells and fragments, and aircraft debris kept Marines defending the perimeter on edge and sleepless. Even so, the Marines were determined to stay on Guadalcanal. Immediately after the transports withdrew and the disastrous Savo Island battle, platoon leaders were instructed to assemble their squad leaders and ask, "Suppose we had to leave this island, all of us, how would we do it?" There were fears that a Japanese counterattack could defeat the tenuous Marine foothold. A typical response from a squad leader of Company L, 3/5th Marines was, "'Cause we ain't going no wheres until our damn U.S. Navy takes us off this damn place!" (quoted in Marion 2004). The responses were relayed to the staff, assuring them that the troops were staying no matter what.

IJA

For sealift, the Japanese often employed merchant ships, known to the Allies as "Marus" as all had *Maru* following the ship's name, i.e., *Canberra Maru*. The Japanese also used destroyers to make high-speed night runs to deliver troops and supplies. IJA-operated landing barges were heavily relied on to deliver troops and supplies, but they suffered high losses; these included the *Shohatsu* 10m (32ft), *Daihatsu* 14m (46ft), *Moku Daihatsu* 15m (50ft), and *Toku Daihatsu* 17m (56ft). Once ashore, much of the Japanese ammunition and supplies sat in dumps deteriorating or was destroyed by US aircraft. Ammunition and supplies were packaged for cold climates, not the tropics. The Japanese based their ammunition resupply on the *Kaisenbun* (division battle), the amount of ammunition expended in four months of combat with an average of 20 days' active combat per month. This was based on experience in Manchuria against the Russians. This was only a half to a third of that expended by a US division. The calculations became meaningless owing to ammunition sunk in transit, deteriorated ashore, abandoned, and simply unable to be moved to the front. In other words, vastly more had to be shipped than was actually expended.

Debarked Japanese supplies were moved off the beaches and hidden in the jungle. The Japanese challenge was moving them many miles to the front lines. Elsewhere during the war – for example, Southeast Area and the Philippines – the IJA relied heavily on horse-drawn transport, but units deploying to the Pacific gave this up. Typically 1½-ton capacity with two-wheel drive, the few trucks available were used to move supplies off the beaches, but beyond that, everything was man-packed, even artillery. With most villages on the coasts, Guadalcanal's indigenous population had few trails through the jungle; they traveled on the beaches, coastal trails, and outrigger canoes. The Japanese assumed what trails there were would expedite the movement of troops and supplies, but they were nothing more than crude footpaths with felled trees bridging streams and gullies. Japanese marches to reach the American flanks and portions of the inland perimeter were brutally exhausting and took much longer than calculated. Limited ammunition for crew-served weapons was carried. While crew-served weapons could be broken into packhorse loads barely transportable by several men, such undertakings demanded an exhausting effort. Weapons and ammunition were abandoned when the Japanese were pursued by the Marines or the ammunition had been expended. It proved impossible to evacuate the large numbers of wounded. Those unable to walk were abandoned.

In terms of morale, the IJA held an extremely lofty view of itself owing to its perceived spiritual superiority. The Japanese soldier relied on two

Marines swim beside the Japanese transport, *Kinugawa Maru*. She was intentionally run aground on November 15, 1942 along with three other transports. They were attacked by Marine coast defense guns, Navy aircraft, and the destroyer USS *Meade* (DD-602). Some 2,000 troops, 260 cases of ammunition, and 1,500 rice bags came ashore, but much ammunition and rations were lost. (USMC Historical Center)

武運長久

敵撃蔵皇軍必勝

祝出征

Small national flags (*hokobukuro*) were frequently carried by Japanese soldiers to enhance good fortune and patriotic virtue. They were traditionally inscribed by friends and family with sentiments of good luck and victory slogans. They were often wrapped around the waist beneath the tunic and carried in backpacks. The flags were highly sought-after souvenirs. (© IWM FLA 5503)

sources of strength: the strength of individual will (*seishin*) derived from physical and mental conditioning, and the national quest to expand the Empire, the Spirit of Yamato (*Yamato-damashii*). This was coupled with the concept of *bushido* (way of the warrior), a discipline developed by the samurai between the 9th and 12th centuries. The samurai no longer existed, but their traditions and values did in the Japanese officer class. They strongly believed that such spiritual superiority would prevail over material superiority and numbers. By the time of October's Matanikau Counteroffensive, however, the Japanese troops on Guadalcanal were suffering the effects of the island's terrain and climate. Even those troops recently arrived were exhausted, the long sea voyages with poor food and the even more restricted diet ashore having worn them down. Malaria and dysentery – *Ga Tō* sickness – hit them hard. Many troops had contracted malaria in Java, the Philippines, or Borneo. Others had to abandon bombed ships and swim ashore, losing their equipment. Their next ordeal was to negotiate the mud-slick Maruyama Trail over ridges, gorges, and streams bridged by paired logs in stifling heat and humidity. The single-file trail, 35 miles long, was laboriously hand-cut by engineers. From Kokumbona it ran far south, turned east to cross the Matanikau River, curved south of Mount Austen, crossed the Lunga, and swung northeast to the Marine perimeter in the vicinity of the fateful Edson's Ridge. The Japanese artillery pieces had to be disassembled and carried, with scores of men relieving the carriers. Components were lowered by rope down steep ravines. Each infantryman carried an artillery round and 12 days' lean rations. The rain was so heavy that units were delayed and much of the artillery abandoned, being impossible to carry on the steep, muddy trail. Seeing gun parts on the trailside – all the 7.5cm Type 41 infantry guns were abandoned – soldiers discarded artillery rounds and even packs. In days the uniforms of the men of the Maruyama Force were in tatters and their open sores and scratches were infected. They went to half-rations as they were behind schedule. Drinkable water was scarce in spite of the rains. They foraged for bamboo sprouts, coconuts, taro, and potatoes. Cooking fires were not permitted at night. They often moved well after nightfall, stumbling on roots, rocks, and mud. Troops smeared luminous insects on the packs in front of them so as not to become separated. Sgt Hara Hisakichi would write in his diary, "We have not yet engaged in battle with the enemy. Dying here would be dying in vain." He also optimistically recorded, "Soon we [would] feast on Yankee food!" (quoted in Jersey 2007: 274–75).

The Battle of the Tenaru

August 19–21, 1942

BACKGROUND TO BATTLE

In the days following the August 7 landings the Marines established their beachhead defense to face the anticipated Japanese counterlanding. The perimeter's flanks were also well defended, but the line extended inland only a short distance. The inland (southern) side of the perimeter, considered too dense for the Japanese to make their way through, was only secured by outposts and patrols. The airfield, dubbed Henderson Field, was operational on August 12, but aircraft did not arrive until the 20th, forming what would become known as the "Cactus Air Force." Japanese air attacks intensified. In the meantime the Marines aggressively patrolled the beachhead's flanks, especially to the west, which was secured by the 5th Marines. The original Japanese airfield troops were concentrated between Matanikau River – 4 miles west of the perimeter – and Kokumbona village. It was from that direction that the Americans expected Japanese reinforcements from the north to arrive. Numerous small patrol actions occurred and one instance, a patrol led by LtCol Frank B. Goettge, 1st MarDiv D-2 (intelligence officer), was delivered by landing craft on August 12 to

The 3rd Defense Battalion had responsibility for defending the American perimeter's beach from Japanese counterlandings and the airfield from air attack. The battalion had two batteries, each with 24 of these .50-cal M2 water-cooled machine guns. (USMC Historical Center)

The 1st Marines existed as the 2nd Advanced Base Regiment in 1913–16; it was redesignated the 1st Regiment then deactivated. It was reactivated during 1917–24, 1925–31, and again on March 1, 1941 from 5th and 7th Marines cadres and assigned to the 1st MarDiv. The 2/1st Marines' positions on the Ilu River were not fully developed and less than two weeks had been spent preparing them with inadequate materials and tools. This communications bunker is typical of the fighting positions. It had no overhead cover other than corrugated sheet steel and dried-out palm fronds. (Tom Laemlein/Armor Plate Press)

locate a Japanese willing to surrender. The "Goettge Patrol" was virtually wiped out, with Goettge himself being killed. Several company and multicompany probes were made into the area, resulting in some sharp actions. Examination of Japanese uniforms indicated some of the troops encountered were recent arrivals.

Throughout this period the Japanese conducted numerous high-level bomber raids on Henderson Field with nightly nuisance attacks to keep the Marines awake and edgy – "Washing-machine Charley" – usually Mitsubishi G4M twin-engine "Betty" bombers. On August 18 Lt-Gen Hyakutake's 17th Army on Rabaul launched Operation *Ka*. The Japanese command was convinced the Allied landing was a secondary operation as no American reinforcements had arrived since the landing. In the first of three major Japanese attempts to dislodge the Marines from their lodgment, the Japanese would employ the Ichiki Detachment (*Ichiki Butai*), an elite IJA force built around the II/28th Infantry (Maj Kuramoto Nobuo). The 1,250-man 28th Infantry Regiment (7th Division), commanded by Col Ichiki Kiyonao, had been assigned to assault Midway in May. After the Midway defeat, the regiment was sent to Guam. While en route back to Japan, it was ordered to Truk owing to the American landing on Guadalcanal. Arriving on August 12, it was attached to the 35th Infantry Brigade, itself on Palau. The Ichiki Detachment's 1st Echelon would be landed from destroyers on the night of August 18/19 at Taivu Point, 19 miles east of the beachhead. This would be an IJN operation and the 8th Fleet had operational control of the involved IJA units. There were concerns within the Japanese command, however. Rear Admiral Tanaka Raizo, commanding the 2nd Destroyer Squadron overseeing the Tokyo Express operations, had overseen numerous landings in the Philippines and Netherlands East Indies; he thought there was too little time to make adequate preparations and discovered a great deal of confusion within the inexperienced staff of the newly established 8th Fleet.

On the date of the Japanese landing at Taivu Point, the Marine perimeter was thinly held. From west to east: the 3/5th Marines secured the west end of the beachhead and refused its left flank 600yd inland; the 1/5th Marines defended Lunga Point and Lunga River estuary; the 3/1st Marines defended the central portion of the beachhead, along with the 1st Special Weapons and 3rd Defense battalions; the 2/1st Marines was positioned on the beachhead's east end and turning inland along the Ilu River (then thought to be the Tenaru) for 3,200yd. This was three times the maximum frontage assigned to a battalion and that was exclusive of 1,500yd of beachfront. Companies E and F, 2/1st Marines were on the line with all platoons up; Company G was battalion reserve. Two observation posts were about 1,000yd to the east.

LtCol Leonard B. Cresswell's 1/1st Marines was held in division reserve near the airfield, but also lightly secured the eastern inland flank with patrols and observation posts (OPs). The 1st Aviation Engineer and 1st Pioneer battalions maintained outposts along the southern inland perimeter and the Lunga River. The 1st Amphibian Tractor Battalion served as a mobile reserve near the western portion of the perimeter and the 1st Light Tank Battalion did the same near the airfield. The inland perimeter near the west flank was "exposed," but the vegetation was so dense to be near impenetrable. Patrols, mainly from the 3/5th Marines on the perimeter's west flank, watched over this area. Regiments often had only a reserve company rather than a battalion.

On the Ilu the 1st Marines constructed field fortifications, cleared fields of fire, and improved the roads and bridges behind the lines. However, by August 18, only limited progress had been made. There was little barbed wire, it having been left aboard the transports. Some wire was recovered from cattle fences behind the plantations. A single-strand tripwire ran on the river's east side. The Americans suspected an enemy force had landed to the east and might attack. However, it was possible only small Japanese elements were to the east and a larger force might attack from another direction or even from the sea. LtGen Vandegrift considered committing the division reserve (1/1st Marines) eastward to engage any enemy force before the Japanese took the initiative and attacked on their own terms. The danger was that the enemy force might be larger than the Marine battalion, even if the latter was in the area. Such action would commit the Marines' reserve and it would not be available if the Japanese attacked from elsewhere. The other course of action open to the Americans was simply to stay in position, continue improving the defenses, and wait for the enemy to attack, someplace. There was good intelligence indicating the Japanese were concentrating to the east, but not enough to justify committing the reserve in an offensive action. MajGen Vandegrift chose to wait. The Marines would not have to wait long.

The Ichiki Detachment's 1st Echelon with 917 men had departed Truk aboard six destroyers on August 16 and landed at Guadalcanal's Taivu Point (known as *Tiabo Misaki* to the Japanese) at 0100hrs on the 19th with 250 rounds of ammunition and seven days' rations per man. They were ferried ashore by landing craft of the 3rd Company, 1st Independent Shipping Engineer Regiment, whose 160 men had been delivered earlier by the Tokyo Express. It was 22 miles via the coastal road to the Ilu River. All supplies and ammunition had to be moved by hand. At the same time, 250 men of the 5th Yokosuka SNLF came ashore at Kokumbona village 7 miles west of the Marine perimeter as a diversion, and three Japanese destroyers bombarded Tulagi Island. The Ichiki Detachment's 1st Echelon was to be followed in four days by its 1,411-man 2nd Echelon, and the 35th Infantry Brigade in ten days. Choosing not to wait for the 2nd Echelon, however, Ichiki immediately moved eastward with 800 men, leaving about 100 to secure the Taivu Point base.

Japanese troops transfer from a destroyer or patrol vessel (destroyer-transport) into a *Daihatsu* landing barge, which could carry up to 70 troops or 10 tons of cargo. They were supplied with kapok life vests, which they would leave in the barge when debarking. (USMC Historical Center)

MAP KEY

1 Dawn, August 19: Company A, 1/1st Marines dispatches a patrol to Koli Point.

2 1300hrs, August 19: Ichiki's advanced party, dispatched at 0830hrs, is engaged and destroyed – bar three survivors – by Company A, 1/1st Marines.

3 Day, August 20: The 1/1st Marines is released from division reserve and deploys as a counterattack force south of the 2/1st Marines.

4 Night, August 20: The 2/1st Marines' two outposts east of the Ilu withdraw. The II/28th Infantry moves into its assembly area.

5 Early morning, August 21: Ichiki's 1st Engineer Company conducts inadequate reconnaissance; his 2nd Machine Gun Company and the Gun Platoon deploy their weapons, and the Japanese rifle companies move into attack positions.

6 0200hrs, August 21: 2nd Company, II/28th Infantry launches its attack across the Ilu sandbar into Company E, 2/1st Marines and elements of Battery B, 1st Special Weapons Battalion. Within a half-hour the Japanese attack is broken and the 2nd Company virtually wiped out, although they take a few Marine foxholes.

7 0245hrs, August 21: The American battalion reserve, Company G, 2/1st Marines, is deployed to reinforce Company E and take back the captured foxholes.

8 0300hrs, August 21: 3rd Company, II/28th Infantry launches a second attack across the sandbar and is quickly wiped out. The 1st Engineer Company also attacks, wading the Ilu 200yd upstream, and is likewise destroyed. Counterattacking, Company E, 2/1st Marines has eliminated most Japanese on the west bank.

9 0445hrs, August 21: Ichiki pulls his command post back 200yd and orders a third attack. The Marines consolidate their positions and distribute ammunition.

10 0500hrs, August 21: 1st Company, II/28th Infantry, after wading beyond the surf line and past the sandbar, attacks into Company E's beach flank. The Japanese attack is shattered.

11 Early morning, August 21: Firing continues through the morning by both sides. The Marines plan a counterattack and the 1/1st Marines moves into position to cross the upper Ilu. Company C, 1st Engineer Battalion reinforces the 2/1st Marines and improves the defenses in the event of a follow-on attack. The 3/5th Marines moves into the area between the airfield and the Ilu to clear out any infiltrators.

12 0700hrs, August 21: The 1/1st Marines crosses the upper Ilu to counterattack the Japanese flank.

13 0900hrs, August 21: The 1/1st Marines crosses the line of departure; Companies A and C attack the Japanese on the sandbar. Company B swings farther east and engages a platoon at the Block Four River.

14 1100hrs, August 21: Company B, 1/1st Marines destroys the Japanese breaking out of the sandspit.

15 1400hrs, August 21: The Japanese survivors are contained on the sandspit between the 2/1st and 1/1st Marines.

16 1500hrs, August 21: A platoon of Company A, 1st Light Tank Battalion crosses the sandbar with covering infantry fire support and wipes out the remaining Japanese. At 1700hrs the east bank of the Ilu is cleared and declared secure by the Marines.

Battlefield environment

The weather was overcast and it rained on and off day and night. The nights were extremely dark. For the Japanese the 22-mile, two-day march was difficult, the men being fully loaded with rations, ammunition, and weapons. Most of the march was conducted on the coastal road or through coconut-palm plantations on level ground. Their approach to the Ilu River offered little concealment, being in a coconut plantation devoid of underbrush.

The Marines' (west) side of the river was also in the plantation, but the upper Ilu on both sides was forested. Brush was on the bank of both sides of the 80–95yd-wide river. The banks were low, but on the Marine side overlooking the sandbar was a piece of raised ground. The sandbar, exposed at low tide and easily wadeable then, was 7–15yd wide when exposed. The sandspit on the east side of the mouth was quite exposed to Marine frontal and flanking fire from numerous machine guns and canister-firing 37mm AT guns backed by mortars and howitzers. The current was slow, but too deep to wade. Swimming with weapons and equipment was almost impossible for most Japanese. The river was an effective obstacle reinforced only by a single-strand tripwire with grenade booby traps on the east side.

While the sandy and crushed limestone soil was relatively easy to dig in, the coconut-palm root systems made it difficult. The system consisted of hundreds of finger-thick fibrous roots 2–3ft below ground and densely radiating 20–30ft. These had to be hacked through with much effort.

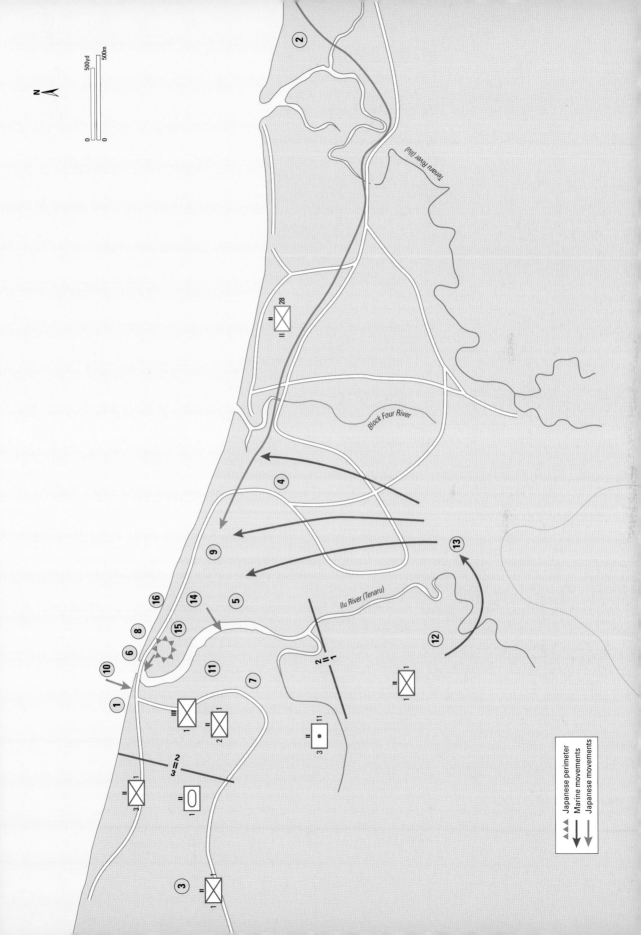

N

500yd
500m

Tenaru River (Ilu)

28

Block Four River

4

9

13

16

14

5

Ilu River (Tenaru)

8

15

6

12

10

11

7

1

2
II
1

1

II
1

1

2

2
II
3

1

II
3

1

3
II
1

1

1

3

2
II
3

II
3

1

1

3

Japanese perimeter
Marine movements
Japanese movements

INTO COMBAT

The Marines began receiving reports from natives and coastwatchers of fresh Japanese troop sightings. Setting off at 0700hrs on the 19th, Capt Charles H. Brush, Jr. of Company A, 1/1st Marines led a 60-man patrol with four native guides 7 miles along the coastal road toward Koli Point. At 0830hrs Ichiki dispatched a 34-man detail under his signals officer, Capt Yoshimi Shibuya, to reconnoiter Marine positions, lay a telephone line, and establish a forward base. After noon, Brush's patrol discovered the Japanese moving in the vegetation between the beach and road with poor security. The Marines killed 31 Japanese including four officers in an hour-long firefight. The Marine main body pinned the Japanese frontally while a platoon outflanked them. The Marines suffered three dead and three wounded. Uniforms indicated the enemy were IJA personnel and not straggler IJN construction or SNLF troops who had been encountered earlier. They recovered a radio code sheet for a landing operation and found extremely accurate sketch maps of Marine dispositions around Henderson Field – made by Japanese observers on Mount Austen. Unfortunately, the documents gave no indication of the Japanese main body's strength or plans.

Three wounded Japanese survivors returned to the main body. Ichiki was rattled that they had been discovered and decided to attack immediately, before the Marines reacted. He dispatched the reinforced 1st Company – the II/28th Infantry's companies are inexplicably recorded as 1st–4th rather than 5th–8th – to find any survivors and secure the route for the main body. They found only dead comrades. Leaving the 1st Platoon, 4th Company behind to bury the dead – it did not take part in the coming battle – Ichiki's force marched all night to reach the Ilu, halting 9 miles short of the river at 0430hrs on the 20th and hiding out during the day. At dusk, the Japanese moved toward the Ilu. The Japanese approach along the coast road meant they had to cross the Tenaru River (mistakenly called the Ilu), some 2 miles from the actual Ilu, and then the smaller Block Four River about a mile before they reached the Ilu. The Japanese swung inland, bypassing the wider and deep mouths of the Tenaru and Block Four rivers. Ichiki feared the old British-built bridges might be guarded. A lead engineer patrol reconnoitered the stream- and river-crossing sites. Ichiki's initial reconnaissance surprised him by revealing that the Marines were as far east as the Ilu. Overall, his reconnaissance was inadequate. The Japanese also greatly underestimated Marine strength. Besides deploying far too small an attack force, the Japanese had no reserve to exploit any successes and certainly no large follow-on force to deal with the rest of the Marine defenders.

On the evening of August 20, Marine listening posts east of the Ilu heard movement and voices. The listening posts crept back to the 2/1st Marines' Ilu positions crossing the sandbar at the river's mouth. The battalion was 100 percent alert. The reserve battalion stood ready as did the other reserves: the tankers, amtracs, engineers, and pioneers. The artillery battalions plotted concentrations to the east. Three 75mm howitzer batteries were positioned just behind the perimeter west of the Ilu. The entire perimeter was ready for action to include the beach defenses. The Marines had dug two- and three-man foxholes 20–30ft from the riverbank. They fixed bayonets at night ready to take on infiltrators. Grenades were ready on the lip of their holes along with spare clips. They were not to shoot at mere noises. If certain the enemy was creeping toward them, they were to use a grenade as it would not reveal their positions. They were directed not to leave their holes unless ordered as they might be shot or grenaded by neighbors. Midnight passed, though, and nothing more happened.

Ichiki arrived at about 0030hrs and directed Maj Kuramoto to attack at 0200hrs. Ichiki was not deterred by a night attack; he had lectured on the subject at the IJA Infantry School. His plan was to punch through the Marine line, occupy the 11th Construction Unit's old camp between the Ilu and Lunga rivers, and launch attacks to seize the airfield and drive the Marines from their positions. This was a rather ambitious plan for only 800 troops, even if there had been only 7,000 Marines on the island as the Japanese mistakenly estimated. The Ichiki Detachment and a single Marine battalion were roughly equal in strength, about 930 men at this time, but the Japanese would attack against two Marine battalions rather than with the normal three-to-one attack ratio. Regardless of the Japanese practice of attacking with unfavorable force ratios but reinforced by surprise, Ichiki's men would be seriously outgunned. A Marine battalion fielded more firepower in all categories and the 2/1st Marines was reinforced by two 37mm AT guns and .50-cal machine guns of Battery B, 1st Special Weapons Battalion, along with its own battalion-level and attached regimental 37mm guns. The Marines defending the beachhead's east flank were supported by 24 75mm and 12 105mm howitzers manned by the 2nd, 3rd, and 5th Battalions, 11th Marines. Barrage concentrations were registered on the east side of the Ilu and especially on the sandbar. The two engaged Marine battalions together fielded eight 81mm and 12 60mm mortars. The Japanese possessed no artillery other than the two 7cm infantry guns organic to the battalion, a weapon roughly equal to the Marine's 81mm mortar in range and projectile weight, but with a slower rate of fire.

It was overcast, moonless, and raining on and off, a pitch-black night. On both sides of the Ilu the terrain was flat and covered with grass, some scattered brush clumps, and palms. On the west side, south of the stream junction, was a dense forest stretching inland. The generally clear fields followed the narrow stream on the east (Japanese) side, but merged into dense forest within 1,000yd of the stream. The men of the 2/1st Marines were dug in along the west bank of the Ilu River. (The flight path of aircraft taking off from Henderson Field flew directly over the river's mouth and the D-Day Beach Red was east of the mouth.) The river was only a few feet deep and the brush-covered banks 3–5ft high. The American-held west bank was slightly higher than the east. Overlooking the sandbar was an 8–10ft-high sand hillock, a natural fortification. The sandbar, 7–15yd wide, could be waded at high tide and was exposed at low tide. (River mouth sandbars are created by the river's outflow current meeting the incoming ocean high-tide surge and surf.) The river was 95yd wide near its mouth and 35yd where it began to narrow and a smaller winding stream joined it from the west. At that point it narrowed down to a stream, 20–25yd wide and winding inland. The wider portion of

An 81mm M1 mortar crew prepares to drop an M43 light HE round down the tube. Each USMC rifle battalion had four mortars in the weapons company's mortar platoon. Within minutes the mortars could be dropping rounds on pre-plotted targets in front of any of the battalion's rifle companies. Japanese rice bags made of woven straw protect this position, which is camouflaged by cut weeds. (Tom Laemlein/Armor Plate Press)

The 2nd Machine Gun Company, 28th Infantry set up 12 7.7mm Type 92 (1932) heavy machine guns on the east side of the river to support the attack. The weapons were fed by 30-round feed strips. The 122lb weapon had carrying bars that fit into the front tripod legs, which are still in-place here. Ten were captured, the others probably lost in the river. (Tom Laemlein/Armor Plate Press)

the river stretched 1,300yd inland in a flattened "S" curve to the junction where it narrowed to 20–25yd. The Marines' prepared defenses were along this portion to about 600yd south of the stream intersection – almost 2,000yd defended.

When the 1/1st Marines was released back to the regiment it took over the sector from a point about 150yd south of the stream junction. Most of this sector lacked prepared defenses. The 2/1st Marines was also responsible for almost 1,400yd of beach. Company E defended the northern portion of the Ilu River line – as well as deploying a platoon on the beach – and Company F the southern. Some 100 men of the 1st Special Weapons Battalion reinforced the beach and sandbar area. Capt James F. Sherman's Company G, 2/1st Marines was in reserve. The 2/1st Marines' weapons company – H – deployed two machine-gun platoons on the river line and a third on the beach. American machine guns were set up with fixed crisscrossing lines aimed down the river's turns to provide final protective fires. At least a dozen machine guns defended this sector.

Ichiki and Kuramoto quietly moved the assault companies forward in column formation. The four 105-man rifle companies – 1st, 2nd, and 3rd with 105 men each, 80 fewer than normal, and 4th Company (lacking its 1st Platoon) fielding about 70 – deployed along with 150 men of the 1st Engineer Company, less its 4th Platoon and material section. The engineers were attached from the 7th Division's battalion-sized 7th Engineer Regiment. Like US engineers, Japanese engineers could fight as infantry and were trained in close assault, breaching obstacles, and defeating fortifications. They were armed as a rifle company plus had flamethrowers. The 2nd Machine Gun Company (110 men) was in support along with the infantry-gun platoon (50 men). Only 23 men of the battalion HQ were present along with part of the Ichiki Detachment HQ. This was made up of 164 regimental HQ, signals, service, and medical personnel, but most were left at the base or had been killed in the earlier engagement.

Much of the Ichiki Detachment's personnel funneled onto a peninsula-like sandspit – AKA "coconut grove" – on the east side of the Ilu. It was flat, sandy ground with scattered palms and trees offering little cover and concealment other than darkness. This was the same piece of ground the men of the 1/5th Marines had bivouacked on during their first night on Guadalcanal. The wide portion of the Ilu would be difficult to cross owing to its depth and width. Wading soldiers would be totally exposed. It also provided the Marines a clear field of fire. The Japanese infantrymen dropped their backpacks, fixed bayonets, checked grenades, ensured they had full magazines, and tightened helmet chinstraps. The Japanese were comparatively well fed, having just arrived on the island, and had been able to find some fresh vegetables from the local population's gardens while en route to the Ilu. On the other hand, the Marines had been on half-rations for two weeks with inadequate nourishment while constructing fighting positions, carrying out work details, and conducting patrols. American rations were Japanese rice and canned fish with occasional greasy C-rations. Nor were the Marines fully acclimatized, having come from New Zealand. Malaria, dysentery, and diarrhea were manifesting themselves on both sides.

The 1/1st Marines was held in division reserve near the northeast end of the airfield. With a Japanese attack imminent, the battalion had been released to 1st Marines control and positioned on the 2/1st Marines' south flank. It was not dug in to extend the Ilu River main line of resistance inland, but positioned to counterattack. Col Cates could deploy the 1/1st Marines either to counterattack into the 2/1st Marines sector to drive out enemy lodgments and restore the Ilu defense line, or to attack into the south (left) Japanese flank. The Marines could only occasionally hear the Japanese stealing toward them. They moved relatively silently as there was little underbrush to make noise. They were Ichiki's lead engineer patrol. The men of Company E, 2/1st Marines could hear even less as noises were covered by surf.

The fully alert Marines awaited the inevitable. It came at 0200hrs (0130hrs in some accounts) when a green flare was fired. Japanese machine guns and grenade dischargers opened fire. The Japanese 2nd Company charged across the sandspit, making for the sandbar and screaming 'Banzai!' Marine riflemen fired at moving shapes and at first BAR-men squeezed off single shots so as not to reveal the locations of the automatic weapons. As it became apparent this was a serious attack, the Marines increased their fire with the BAR-men switching to full-automatic. Machine guns opened up as did the 60mm and 81mm mortars. The 75mm howitzers of the 3/11th Marines began firing illumination. (Mortar illumination rounds were not yet available.) The drifting parachute-suspended flares cast a maze of crisscrossing tree shadows. Each flare cast its own set of shadows, resulting in confusing shadows moving in opposing directions and making it difficult to detect movement on the ground.

Machine guns hammered out streams of red tracers ricocheting off the river's surface and trees. US machine guns and AT guns were sited to fire down the length of the sandbar and sandspit to enfilade the swarming enemy. This position on the west end of the Ilu sandbar was dubbed "Hell's Point" owing to the extent of Japanese fire it drew. Three Company H machine-gunners received the Navy Cross for holding their exposed position. The 37mm AT guns blasted canister rounds into the teeming Japanese. One 37mm fired onto the sandbar from the flank to be especially devastating. Each round spit out 122 ⅜in lead balls. The shotgun-like canister ruptured within 30yd and was effective up to 250yd. The lead Japanese were caught in the wire on the sandbar's west, cutting the wire or leaping over it. In spite of devastating fire, small numbers overran a few Marine positions in hand-to-hand fights. A Japanese LMG crew swam the river and set up in an abandoned amtrac to knock out the defilading 37mm. It was taken over by Marines who were unfamiliar with it, but got it firing again. Even though the Marines were outnumbered in the immediate vicinity of the sandbar, their firepower chewed the enemy to pieces – they held.

A Marine poses with one of the 7cm Type 92 (1932) infantry gun (*daitaiho*) with tool and parts kits captured at the Ilu River. Either two or four equipped the infantry battalion's gun platoon/company. Four of its black-painted HE rounds were carried in the metal container to the right. Note the comparatively short cartridge case. A marginally effective AP (armor-piercing) and a white smoke shell were also available. (Tom Laemlein/Armor Plate Press)

The 1st Light Tank Battalion's Companies A and B were equipped with M2A4 light tanks and Company C with M3 light tanks. Here, two M2A4s with an M3 between them move toward the Matanikau River. The infantryman standing behind the lead tank's turret serves as a guide. The yellow band around the turret was to identify the tank as American as the small star was not sufficiently obvious. Platoons were identified by a small geometric shape on the turret (circle, square, triangle), but it is not known which shape identified each platoon. A number in the symbol indicated the company (1 = HQ, 2 = A, and so on). There were 18 tanks to a company – three platoons of five and three in the company HQ. The tanks were held in reserve to be deployed to endangered sectors if necessary. Each light tank had a Thompson M1928A1 submachine gun as "on-vehicle equipment." (Tom Laemlein/Armor Plate Press)

LtCol Edwin A. Pollock, commanding the 2/1st Marines, committed his reserve, Company G, less than an hour into the fight – before Ichiki launched his second attack. The troops reinforced the line and wiped out the Japanese who had taken over foxholes. Pollock's decision to commit his reserve was well timed. If he had waited until the main assault was defeated before taking back the occupied positions and strengthening the line, he would have had a tougher time dealing with the Japanese footholds while also contending with what was coming next. Pollock "was seen bending low while moving along the line of riflemen, telling everyone in his calm and competent way, to 'stay low, sight your target and squeeze 'em off'" (Jersey 2007: 211).

At 0230hrs Ichiki launched his second attack. The 3rd Company followed in the 2nd Company's tracks and was likewise cut to pieces on the sandbar. At the same time the 1st Engineer Company assaulted a couple of hundred yards upstream. Wading the river, they did not have a chance and were quickly cut down and the few survivors fled. They did manage to knock out a 37mm. Both Japanese companies were cut to ribbons. A 3rd Company officer returning to Ichiki's command post begged for the survivors to be withdrawn. Ichiki refused and prepared a third assault. While this was under way, Marine artillery and mortars barraged the east side of the Ilu within 100yd of the defenders to hamper the regrouping Japanese. At 0445hrs, Ichiki pulled his command post back 200yd from the sandspit and readied for yet another attack.

Company E had only one platoon, reinforced by machine guns and AT guns, defending the beach. Ichiki followed the defeat of the cross-river assaults with a surprise. The 1st Company waded beyond the surf line, making its way past the river mouth. Ichiki saved this company for the last as it was prewar practice to assign the best troops to the 1st Company. Ichiki's two feeble 7cm infantry guns opened fire as did 5cm grenade dischargers. These few weapons firing into such a wide area had little effect on the dug-in Marines other than a few casualties. At 0500hrs the 1st Company charged out of the surf and onto the beach just past the sandbar outflanking the barbed wire. They were cut down in droves by US machine guns, mortars, and artillery. Few escaped the cauldron. There were exchanges of rifle and machine-gun fire through the rest of the night. Dawn found dozens of Japanese half-buried in high tide-washed sand. Japanese on the east side of the river were mainly concentrated on the sandspit at the Ilu's mouth. Regardless of hundreds of his force having been cut down, Ichiki refused to withdraw, however. (The 4th Company is not mentioned in records. Its two platoons may have been split up between other companies or held in reserve.)

Col Gerald C. Thomas, 1st MarDiv D-3 (operations), stated, "We aren't going to let those people lay up there all day" (quoted in Frank 1992: 154). Before dawn, Col Cates decided to counterattack to clear the river's east bank. Crossing the sandbar or the wider river portion below it was ruled out. The 1/1st Marines would move south and cross the Ilu on the narrow upstream portion and then swing north into the Japanese flank. While the battalion was preparing, Company C, 1st Aviation Engineer Battalion reinforced the 2/1st Marines and constructed AT obstacles, laid mines, strung wire, and helped improve fighting positions. Japanese snipers harassed the Marines as they worked. Cates had no idea if a larger force was readying for another attack. In the meantime, the 3/5th Marines was directed to move into the area between the airfield and the Ilu to sweep up any infiltrating Japanese. None had made it that far.

At 0700hrs the 1/1st Marines crossed the upper Ilu and took position to roll into the Japanese flank. LtCol Cresswell positioned the weapons company's HMGs to cover escape routes to the south (inland). At 0900hrs the rifle companies crossed the line of departure with Companies A and C attacking the flank and rear of the Japanese compressed onto the sandspit. Company B swung farther east to cut off the enemy's retreat toward the Tenaru (then mistakenly known as the Ilu). In the vicinity of the Block Four River mouth, Company C engaged a withdrawing platoon-sized group. They isolated it and wiped it out. Company A met little resistance as it pushed remnants onto the sandspit. Some Japanese attempted to flee through the surf or down the beach. One group broke out to the east, but ran into Company C advancing from the Block Four firefight.

Grumman F4F Wildcat fighters of VMF-223, which had arrived the day before, began launching from Henderson Field, flying directly over the river mouth and circling back to strafe the sandspit and any fleeing enemy. They also strafed Japanese barges bringing preplanned supplies down the coast from Taivu Point to reinforce Ichiki's expected success. Skirmishes and firefights continued through the day with repeated Japanese attempts to break out. By 1400hrs, the remaining Japanese were contained on the sandspit. The Company G CO ordered his troops to cease firing and wasting ammunition on Japanese in the surf. GySgt Charlie Angus, experienced in competitive shooting, selected a position and relentlessly picked off the bobbing survivors.

Col Cates needed to finish off the Japanese survivors before dark when they could escape. At 1500hrs he ordered a platoon of five M2A4 tanks under 1Lt Leo B. Case of Company A, 1st Light Tank Battalion to "reconnoiter" across the sandbar. One struck a mine and another mired in soft sand. The other three rumbled through the palms firing 37mm canister and blasting away with their five machine guns. The tanks rolled over dead and living Japanese without mercy. The survivors fought back with magnetic AT charges and grenades. None willingly surrendered. Fifteen Japanese prisoners, only two of whom were unwounded, were collected; most were found unconscious by souvenir- and food-hunting Marines. War correspondent Richard W. Tregaskis recorded:

> We watched these awful machines as they plunged across the spit and into the edge of the grove. It was fascinating to see them bustling amongst the

The II/28th Infantry was virtually wiped out on the Ilu River and during its attempted withdrawal. Few needed the ammunition in their two-30-round cartridge boxes, much less the 60 rounds of rifle ammunition held in the reserve cartridge box on the back of the belt. (Tom Laemlein/Armor Plate Press)

trees, pivoting, turning, spitting sheets of yellow flame. It was like a comedy of toys, something unbelievable to see them knocking over palm trees which fell slowly, flushing the running figures of men from underneath their treads, following and firing at the fugitives. (Quoted in Frank 1992: 155)

MajGen Vandegrift said it more brusquely: "… the rear of the tanks looked like meat grinders" (quoted in Jersey 2007: 212). The Ilu east bank was declared secure at 1700hrs.

The Marines lost 35 dead and 63 wounded (74 in some accounts), of whom half were soon returned to duty. The seriously wounded were evacuated to Efate Island via USS *Colhoun* (APD-2). The Japanese lost almost 800 dead including their commander. One report claimed Ichiki was last seen charging into the fight. Another claimed a Marine shot him when he drew a pistol and another says he committed *seppuku* (ritual suicide) after burning the regimental colors. Only two junior officers and about 30 men, most wounded, reached the Taivu Point base. The Marines recovered approximately 700 rifles, 20 pistols, 20 LMGs, ten HMGs, 20 grenade dischargers, two 7cm infantry guns, 12 flamethrowers (none were discharged), and large numbers of grenades, sabers, and bayonets. Numerous weapons were lost in the surf and river.

This engagement awakened the American realization that the Japanese would literally fight to the death and demonstrated an unheard of degree of tenacity and determination – even when to continue the attack or resist was futile. There were numerous reports of deceptions and ruses such as Japanese playing dead and shooting or grenading Marines. MajGen Vandegrift, a veteran of the vicious Banana Wars and China, said, "I have never heard of this kind of fighting" (quoted in Manchester 1980).

The Ichiki Detachment's 2nd Echelon was still en route aboard slow transports and were informed on August 21:

The news of 14:00, perhaps by enemy radio. *Ichiki-Shitai* landed before daylight on the 18th and advanced to the airfield, enemy reinforcements landed on the 20th on the other side. And we haven't occupied the airfield yet. We estimated *Ichiki-Shitai* will make a night attack tonight, retake and occupy the whole airfield area. They will exterminate all of the enemy on Guadalcanal with the aid of our 2nd Echelon, but our transports are fatally slow! It [was later reported] that *Ichiki-Shitai* had been almost 100 percent exterminated by 9:00 of this day – we didn't know that then. (Inui 1992)

The 2nd Echelon was diverted to Shortland; 128 Japanese survivors remained at Taivu Point. On August 22, the base radioed the 17th Army at Rabaul that the Ichiki Detachment was annihilated short of the airfield. The high command's first reaction was disbelief owing to the low esteem it held for Americans, and would not accept the news until it was confirmed on the 25th. Regardless of the blow, they recovered and persisted with plans to send additional forces and drive the Marines from the island. Rear Admiral Tanaka somberly observed, "This tragedy should have taught the hopelessness of 'bamboo spear' tactics" (quoted in Hough, Ludwig, & Shaw 1958: 291). The belief that Japanese spirit would overcome firepower and material superiority was seriously challenged.

The Henderson Field Attack

September 12–14, 1942

BACKGROUND TO BATTLE

Before the battle of the Tenaru was over, the determined Japanese command implemented plans to commit more troops. They realized the partly finished airfield was the Americans' focus. It would be their Southern Solomons base of operations, allowing them to strike northward to drive the Japanese from the Solomons. The Japanese 17th Army was assigned two divisions, the 2nd and 38th. It was decided instead, however, that two available smaller forces would be immediately dispatched to Guadalcanal. This time the Japanese intended to employ a reinforced brigade fielding five infantry battalions plus the Ichiki Detachment's 2nd Echelon, but the latter would sustain substantial casualties before being reorganized as the Kuma Battalion. On August 21, three Japanese carriers, two battleships, 11 cruisers, 17 destroyers, and a seaplane carrier sortied from Truk heading for the southern Solomons. They would locate the two American carrier groups in the area, attack them, and then engage other naval forces near Guadalcanal. This would be followed by landing reinforcements to retake Guadalcanal. The two fleets would never come in direct contact, but fight one another via air attacks on August 24–25. The battle of the Eastern Solomons delayed Japanese plans for reinforcing Guadalcanal. It also allowed

Following the battle of the Tenaru, the Marine perimeter battalions increased patrols into "Indian Country," especially to the west and east. Here, a USMC company crosses what may be the Ilu River. Obviously the area is considered secure. If not, a squad patrol would cross first covered by automatic weapons, to be followed by the rest of the platoon. It would secure the far side and the remainder of the company would cross with wider intervals between men. Half of the weapons platoon would cross while the other half provided cover and then it would cross when the first half was set up on the far side. (USMC Historical Center)

American supply ships to reach Guadalcanal along with more construction troops. The Marines were still on short rations and had yet to receive any replacements. A thousand men were hospitalized with malaria.

The 2nd Echelon remnants were reorganized into the 658-man Kuma Battalion (*Kuma* means "bear" – the Ainu people of the northern Japanese islands believed the gods visited earth in the guise of bears making them powerful creatures) and attached to the 35th Infantry Brigade. The battalion consisted of: the 1st and 2nd Companies; regimental gun company with four 7.5mm Type 41 guns; antitank company with four 3.7cm Type 94 guns; 8th Independent Antitank Company (armed with German-made 3.7cm PaK 35/36 guns); engineer platoon; and the supply train. Once on Guadalcanal it would absorb the remnants of the 1st Echelon. Only half of the 500 troops of the 5th Yokosuka SNLF troops survived. The 35th Infantry Brigade (AKA the Kawaguchi Detachment, called "Force" in Allied documents) was commanded by Maj-Gen Kawaguchi Kiyotake. It also absorbed the Aoba Detachment with the 4th Infantry Regiment (2nd Division), originally destined for Samoa. Besides five infantry battalions, the brigade was reinforced by ten artillery companies, six AT companies, five AA companies, and a mortar battalion – a significant amount of fire support the Ichiki Detachment had lacked.

The Kawaguchi Detachment would be delivered by destroyers and some barges in the hope they would be less vulnerable to air attack. On August 26 the II/124th Infantry transferred to patrol-vessels at sea to make the first run, followed by the I/124th Infantry. The patrol vessel and barge runs suffered losses, but between August 27 and September 4, much of the brigade – 5,200 troops – landed at Taivu Point. The 1,000 troops transported in 61 barges suffered air attacks and were landed at scattered points. On the night of August 30/31 the 2nd Echelon landed at Tasimboko, 22 miles east of the perimeter near Taivu Point, and the II/124th Infantry near Kokumbona, 8 miles west of the perimeter. The two forces were 30 miles apart. Kawaguchi planned a complex three-pronged attack coordinated with air and naval bombardments. Timing was essential. This was a common Japanese tactic: The main body would attack in the most beneficial sector as flanking units enveloped or encircled the enemy. With Marine defenses tied into the sea, the enemy could not be encircled, but the flanks could be attacked. The flanking attacks were not expected to penetrate the defenses, but were diversions. The idea was to make the American command uncertain which of the three attacks was the main one, delay or confuse committing reserves, and "dilute" the artillery support rather than permitting it all to be concentrated on the main attack. After the main attack's success, the wing units would continue exerting pressure to hold the defenders in place rather than allowing them to turn and face the main attack.

The Right Wing Unit was the Kuma Battalion reinforced by the survivors of the battle of the Tenaru. It would attack the 1/1st Marines, situated almost 4,000yd inland and dug in along the narrow portion of the Tenaru (still called the Ilu). Col Oka Akinosuka's Left Wing Unit included the 124th Infantry, with the 650-man II/124th Infantry to be followed by the 658-man III/4th Infantry hitting the 3/5th Marines near the beach and just inland. Akinosuka's men were backed by 1,200 stragglers of the 11th and 12th Construction units and 450 personnel of the 3rd Kure SNLF. The Kawaguchi Detachment's Main Body – the I/124th, III/124th, and II/4th Infantry – would attack in a column of

Elements of the 4th Infantry Regiment march along the coastal road toward the Ilu River. The III/4th Infantry would support the II/124th Infantry attack on the 3/1st Marines on the west flank and the II/4th Infantry took part in the Edson's Ridge attack with the rest of the 124th Infantry Regiment. The III/4th Infantry was not directly engaged other than suffering losses to artillery. (USMC Historical Center)

battalions into the Raider-Parachute Battalion defending the low ridge complex south of Henderson Field. The Main Body and wing units would be well supported by artillery, mortars, and AT guns, or so it was planned. The ridge and a simple track to guide on led straight to the airfield. If they made it through the Raiders and Paratroopers, ahead of the Japanese were most of the dug-in 1st Pioneer Battalion and the 1st Amphibian Tractor Battalion in their lightly armored tractors sprouting machine guns. Beyond these American troops were the Division HQ, the 11th Marines artillery HQ, and two howitzer batteries. Northwest of the airfield was the division reserve, the 2/5th Marines, with trucks to move them. To the airfield's northeast was the 1st Light Tank Battalion.

For Kawaguchi's Main Body to reach the ridge leading to Henderson Field, they had to cut a trail over the jungle-covered hills, ridges, and gorges. The Japanese engineers began hand-cutting the trail from Tasimboko a few miles west of Taivu Point on September 2 under horrid conditions. To prevent detection, the route had to be masked by terrain. Approaching on the coastal road, they swung inland some miles east of the Ilu River to avoid Marine patrols. Striking southwest, they paralleled the Ilu, crossing it well inland, then cut their way north toward the perimeter for 2,000yd to discover they were still east of the ridge. They cut another trail back to the southeast, curved west, and again approached the ridge just east of the Lunga River. The Right Wing Unit also followed this trail to where it neared the Ilu, which it crossed to reach its attack position. In the meantime the Left Wing Unit marched from Kokumbona avoiding the coastal road altogether and turned inland to reach its position on the Marine west flank. Ridges ran perpendicular to the coast (cross-compartmented terrain), forcing them on a strenuous up-and-down path. Kawaguchi dispatched his units in small groups over a week-long period.

Kawaguchi's plan worked. Marine ground and aerial patrols did not detect the jungle-hidden trail. Marine patrols east and southeast of the perimeter more frequently encountered enemy patrols scouting the defenses. Local inhabitants reported large bodies of troops on the coastal road and in the jungle all moving toward the perimeter, prompting the locals to seek protection within the perimeter. This did not help the American food shortage, but the men were put to work on the airfields. There was Japanese command confusion, though, with the IJN being told the attack would commence on September 11, not the 12th.

The main action of the battle for Henderson Field was centered on Edson's Ridge. Here, a Marine company marches up the fabled ridge. Like most other ridges and hills on Guadalcanal, the tops were covered only by kunai grass and the sides by trees and dense underbrush, allowing attackers to move in close before exposing themselves. The Henderson Field clearing is in the background. (USMC Historical Center)

MAP KEY

1 September 12/13: Having commenced its march from Tassafaronga on the night of September 9/10, the Japanese Left Wing Unit (II/124th and III/4th Infantry) spends a third night reconnoitering the Marine perimeter.

2 Evening, September 13: Following Japanese air raids on Henderson Field at 0950, 1300, and 1730hrs, the II/124th Infantry breaks from march formation into three company columns and deploys to the line of departure.

3 Late evening, September 13: 3rd Platoon, Company L, 3/5th Marines detects Japanese infiltrators and fires on them without reaction.

4 0500hrs, September 14: Men of the 1st Platoon, Company L, 3/5th Marines hear the Japanese approaching.

5 0520hrs, September 14: Two companies of the II/124th Infantry advance in three columns: to the north, a company in column of three platoons; in the center, a company (less one platoon) in column of two platoons; to the south, a detached platoon for right flank security.

6 0525hrs, September 14: The II/124th Infantry launches its attack.

7 0530hrs, September 14: The men of the 1st Platoon, Company L, 3/5th Marines hold their fire until the US 37mm AT gun fires canister. All weapons of Company L open fire on the attackers.

8 0540hrs, September 14: The main Japanese attack on the road and beach is halted in minutes.

9 0550hrs, September 14: The Japanese attack continues on L Company Ridge through the morning. A single squad of the 1st Platoon from the beach reinforces the 3rd Platoon on the ridge.

10 Morning, September 14: The Japanese occupy points on the ridge crest. Most are driven off by small groups of Marines independently counterattacking without artillery or mortar support.

11 Noon, September 14: Using a 60mm mortar and rifle grenades, the Marines drive the remaining Japanese off the ridge, but firing continues all day.

12 Afternoon, September 14: The 1st and 3rd Platoons struggle to re-establish contact between the ridge and beach positions.

13 Night, September 14/15: Firing continues, but no organized Japanese attacks. On the morning of the 15th a US patrol discovers that the Japanese have withdrawn, leaving over 100 dead.

Battlefield environment

Company L, 3/5th Marines found itself defending a challenging piece of terrain. It stretched from the water's edge, through the coconut grove, across the "Copra Cart Trail," through more palms on gently sloping ground, up the end of a low limestone ridge and along the broad V-shaped ridge crest to tie into Company K's positions. The beach was about 20yd wide, with another 10yd through the palms to the road. It was 100yd through the palms on the level, then another 100yd on gradually rising ground to tie into the south arm of a V-shaped ridge. The main US line of defense followed the south ridge crest turning inland for a couple of hundred more yards. Limited construction and barrier materials and tools were available. Today the area is covered by warehouses and a golf course within the island's capital of Honiara.

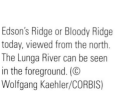

Edson's Ridge or Bloody Ridge today, viewed from the north. The Lunga River can be seen in the foreground. (© Wolfgang Kaehler/CORBIS)

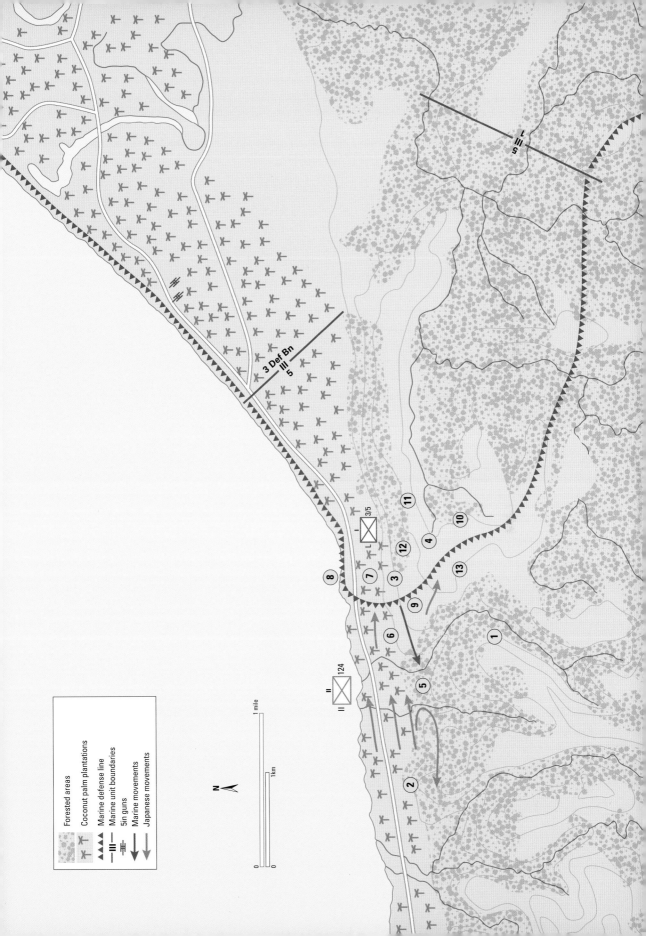

3 Def Bn
III
5

L
III
5

11

3/5
L

12   4

10

8   7   3   13

9

6

1

5

124
II
II

2

Forested areas
Coconut palm plantations
Marine defense line
Marine unit boundaries
5in guns
Marine movements
Japanese movements

N

1 mile
1km

INTO COMBAT

Many books have been written about Bloody Ridge. This study focuses on the lesser action on the Marine west flank. Capt Lyman D. Spurlock's Company L, 3/5th Marines would bear the Left Wing Unit's attack on the night of September 13/14. The parent unit, the 5th Marines, was commanded by Col LeRoy P. Hunt and was the first ashore on Beach Red on August 7. The regiment had originally served in 1917–19, mostly with the Army's 2nd Division in France. It was active in 1920–30 and reactivated on September 1, 1934, assigned to the 1st Marine Brigade in 1935, and to the 1st MarDiv in February 1941.

LtCol Biebush's 3/5th Marines had defended the perimeter's west flank since August 9. A simple sand berm was built across the beach, through the coconut grove, and to the ridge's end. No photographs or detailed description of this berm are available. It was dug with hand tools with the resulting ditch – doubling as a trench – on the inside. It was probably 3–4ft high with irregular firing notches cut in the top. It probably made some modest angular turns rather than following a straight line. The Marines dug out niches in the berm's backside for rifle and BAR positions and the machine-gun positions were reinforced by sandbags and coconut logs. The ridge crest was entrenched in places where the limestone could be dug into or otherwise protected by coconut logs, sandbags, and limestone rocks. Fibrous coconut logs were effective in stopping bullets and absorbing blast and fragmentation. There were only four machine guns in the Company L sector – two air-cooled M1919A4 LMGs and two water-cooled M1917A1 HMGs – with one of each type on the ridge and the other on the lower ground. A 37mm AT gun and an HMG were situated beside the road, thought by the Americans to be the main avenue of attack, which it initially was. Beside the beach and road being an obvious attack route, there were benefits to Company L in being in this sector. They had comparatively clearer fields of observation and fire through the palms and down the road and beach than other perimeter sectors owing to the dense jungle. The beach behind Company L was defended by Company I, 3/5th Marines.

On the MLR within a few hundred yards of shore, the ground was no more than 20ft above sea level covered with palms and grassland. It gradually rose to 80–100ft in the inland forested areas. Spurlock's "Love Company" – companies were informally known by their Phonetic Alphabet words – began its MLR with a 3–4ft sand berm studded with rifle and machine-gun positions 30yd across the beach to the coastal road, what the Marines called the "Copra Cart Trail." The berm continued through the coconut grove for another 100yd

The 11th Marines deployed three battalions of 75mm M1A1 pack howitzers to Guadalcanal – 12 tubes per battalion – range 9,610yd. One 75mm battalion was close behind the Ilu River defensive positions. The "pack 75" could pump out six rounds a minute. At this time the M48 HE projectiles were yellow with black marking. In 1943 they changed to olive drab with black markings. Note the tan burlap sandbags spotted with green paint. This howitzer covers the east end of the perimeter and the Ilu River. (USMC Historical Center)

or so. In the forest the line crawled over gradually rising forested limestone for another 100yd to tie into a flattened V-shaped limestone ridge, which the Americans called "L Company Ridge" – the Japanese called it *Tora Oka* (Tiger Hill). It was virtually impossible to dig into the limestone. Positions were built of rocks, logs, and scarce sandbags on the crest. Being in the open, they were rather exposed and almost impossible to camouflage. The Marines were unable to dig in on the military crest (a line situated below the crest, its location preventing positions from being silhouetted against the sky) owing to its steepness. Biebush's men were familiar with the ground west of their main line of resistance, having constantly reconnoitered the area. The Americans determined Japanese stragglers were organized and dug in between the Matanikau River – 3,500yd beyond the Marine line – and leveled Kokumbona village – 6,000yd beyond the main line of resistance (MLR). The Japanese were on short rations and lightly armed, but potent enough to skirmish with Marine patrols and make it dangerous to cross the 40–50yd-wide Matanikau.

1Lt John "Flash" Flaherty's 1st Platoon, Company L, defended the beach, road, and coconut grove to the end of the ridge. A regimental 37mm gun was dug in beside the road on the beach side with a four-man crew. On the other side of the road was a .30-cal HMG. LMGs and BARs were positioned along the line. 2Lt Edward Farmer's 3rd Platoon with an attached HMG held the ridge, the company's most important part of its sector. The 2nd Platoon – its commander and platoon sergeant had been killed in August – was farther inland on the ridge, tied into Company K. Normally one of the platoons would be in support behind the two on the line. It could reinforce them, secure an exposed flank if the adjacent company was penetrated, or counterattack if the enemy occupied any forward positions. The men who manned night-time listening posts were usually drawn from the support platoon.

Marines in an entrenched position atop a limestone ridge. This could be "L Company Ridge" held by Company L, 3/1st Marines. To the left is a M1919A4 machine gun and the seated Marine holds a Thompson M1928A1 SMG. A five-pocket carrier for magazines is beside his right leg. A shelter-half lies beside the M1919A4 to cover it when it rains. Niches for hand grenades are dug inside the trench's front. (USMC Historical Center)

A single strand of barbed tripwire was within grenade range. C-ration cans were hung on this with a few pebbles as early warning devices – "rattle-traps." If they rattled, a grenade was thrown. Some Marines even practiced with unarmed grenades, which they recovered. In some sectors Marines rigged booby traps by wiring grenades to trees a couple of feet above the ground and setting tripwires. There was five-second delay when the wire was tripped, but this might catch following troops – plus it alerted the Marines. The problem was that the grenade made a faint pop when tripped, thereby alerting the enemy. The Marines also discovered their yellow-painted "pineapples" could easily be detected at night, allowing the Japanese to find them and throw them back. In 1943 grenades began to be painted olive drab.

Marines were taught to clear-cut vegetation for fields of fire. They discovered from the Japanese that vegetation should not be completely cleared as it signaled where weapons were sited and that they had entered a field of fire. Instead, they cut just enough foliage to make approaching troops more visible. The jungle nights were as dark as dark can be – especially when overcast and moonless. Vegetation was just about always wet from rain, mist, or dew. The damp ground vegetation silenced footfalls as did rain. In the flanking positions near the beach the surf further masked sounds. Wildlife had mostly left the area but with the coming of dawn, birds created significant racket. The numerous land crabs and rats were particularly unnerving as they sounded much like a man moving through leaves. Wild pigs and water buffaloes – what Marines mistakenly called "caribous," confusing the name with the Filipino "carabao" – frequently blundered into Marine and Japanese positions, giving their occupants serious scares … and providing meat.

On the 13th, Japanese air raids arrived at 0950hrs, 1300hrs, and 1730hrs. The Cactus Air Force had received another 60 aircraft in the preceding days, but 120 Japanese aircraft arrived at Rabaul. After dark "Louie the Louse" dropped a flare to mark the airfield for Japanese destroyers running through The Slot. At 2100hrs Kawaguchi's Main Body signaled its attack by firing flares, with the I/124th Infantry in the lead and slamming into the Raider-Paras' center and right. The attack went in without artillery preparation. The battle would go on until dawn with the Japanese launching over a dozen attacks. The Japanese threw in what artillery and mortars they could but ammunition was short, as it was for Marine mortars. Some 2,000 rounds of American 105mm were fired. At 0400hrs on the 14th the 2/5th Marines' reserve companies began moving into the Raider-Paras' left.

The Marines manning the rest of the perimeter could hear the heavy firing in the direction of Edson's Ridge and expected a *banzai* charge out of the jungle at any moment. Every man was 100 percent alert. On the Marines' east flank, two companies of the Kuma Battalion (Right Flank Unit) struck the 3/1st Marines from across the Ilu after the Japanese Main Body attacked. They achieved no penetration during the night-long firefight. Three companies of the II/124th Infantry (Left Flank Unit) were approaching Company L, 3/5th Marines on the west flank. The following Japanese unit – the III/4th Infantry, also part of the Left Flank Unit – never joined the fight. Last-minute changes in Japanese plans caused uncoordinated attack times and some elements failed to link up with their parent units after the grueling march.

The Japanese 5cm Type 89 (1929) grenade discharger (*jutekidanto*), or what the Marines called a "knee mortar." It is shown here with a 5cm HE mortar round, but it could also fire Type 97 hand grenades with a special propellant charge attached to the base, plus pyrotechnic signal smoke and flare rounds. (Tom Laemlein/Armor Plate Press)

Some Company L troops had been unloading fuel drums at the airfield and when they returned to their positions in the evening of the 13th were told an attack was expected. They dug in further, checked their ammunition and grenades, and ate a lean meal while listening for rattle-trap sounds. PFC Art Boston of the 3rd Platoon on the ridge fired three rounds at a rattle-trap noise, only to be chewed out by 2Lt Farmer. Boston claimed, "There are Japs down there. I can smell 'em" (quoted in Marion 2004). Alerted again, he fired another shot and was again warned as he was upsetting the troops. At about 0530hrs on the 14th the pre-dawn quiet was shattered by screams of, "Ah, Malines – you die, Ah, Malines you die!" The attackers also yelled "Gas attack, gas attack!" which failed to rattle the waiting Marines. (In this battle it is not known which actions were conducted by specific Japanese companies – the III/124th Infantry consisted of the 7th to 9th companies.) One Japanese company charged through the scattered palms with little cover for protection. The Marines opened fire at a rapid rate. Every machine gun and BAR was streaming tracers into the darkness. The Japanese returned fire with rifles and LMGs. The muzzle flashes, tracers, grenades, mortars, and Japanese flares dissolved the shadows and blinded both sides' troops. The Japanese hit the barbed wire and came to a halt, apparently fearing booby-trapped grenades. They soon pressed on, tearing down and going over or under the wire, and Marines showered grenades on them. The Japanese fired 5cm grenade dischargers, but the Marine fighting positions protected most American personnel. Boston stated, "My rifle got so hot that as soon as I got a round in the chamber, it would go off, before I could pull the trigger [a "cook-off"]" (quoted in Marion 2004).

During the early morning of the 14th the 1st Platoon, covering the beach, road, and coconut grove, heard the Japanese at 150yd out, giving them sufficient time to prepare. The clouds cleared and the Japanese could be seen in the pale moonlight. Two companies came through the palms in three columns, talking and rattling equipment, apparently unaware they were walking into a kill zone. No doubt they were expecting guides to meet them and lead them forward. Without finding the guides, who may have earlier become casualties, they blundered on. Moonlight glinted off the leading officers' swords. In the Marines' eyes the enemy were stupid or arrogant. They assumed the Japanese were used to their opponents fleeing before them as had so often occurred on Sarawak and North Borneo. The Marines were not going anywhere. They knew full well that there was no place to run to: "the only thing we *could* do was fight" (quoted in Marion 2004). They knew there was no company or battalion reserve to back them. The order was relayed, "Hold your fire until our 37mm lets go" (quoted in Marion 2004. The main Japanese group was 25yd from the berm when the 37mm ripped loose with canister – one round was like 122 instantaneous rifle shots making a humming buzz through the massed soldiers. All machine guns and BARs immediately opened up at full rate while riflemen meticulously picked off soldiers trying to flee, leaving those still advancing to the automatic weapons hammering red tracers on their final protective fire lines. The HMGs were

The Japanese Type 92 (1932) steel helmet (*tetsubo*) was made of low-grade steel and was easily penetrated by fragments. The five-pointed star represented the IJA. SNLF troops displayed the anchor device. The suspension liner was leather and the helmet had an elaborate tie-tape system for a chin strap. (© IWM UNI 151)

pre-set to obliquely cross the company's front. Each gun was locked in a designated position in both direction and elevation to fire approximately 1yd above the ground. Their tripods were weighted down with sandbags to provide a stable base. The guns fired at a rapid rate with repeated bursts until the attack was broken. It appears the Japanese failed to position their own HMGs for fire support. Enemy troops literally ran into a dense stream of bullets. At least a dozen canister rounds were fired to decimate the swarming Japanese. Some Japanese attempted to surge to the Marine left flank to avoid the intense fire. They too were cut down. Others panicked and ran into the surf, dropping their weapons.

Behind the disorganized and confused Japanese, Marine 75mm HE rounds along with some 105mm were impacting in near-continuous battery barrages. Retreating Japanese fled into a meat grinder of screaming shrapnel. Closer to the Marine positions, rounds fired from the company's two 60mm and the battalion's four 81mm mortars were detonating on the beach, sending gouts of sand skyward. Some rounds detonated in palm tops to shower a deadly rain on the Japanese below. The 81mm light HE round weighed 6.92lb with 1.22lb of TNT while the 75mm pack howitzer projectile weighed 14.70lb with 1.47lb TNT. The 75mm had a thick steel body twice as heavy as that of an 81mm. It mostly broke up into large fragments that could pass through several men, vehicles, light structures, and similar targets. The 81mm, with only a slightly smaller bursting charge, had a thin body and the charger shattered it into hundreds of small, man-maiming fragments. Soldiers often underplayed the value of their own mortars, but regardless of which side they were on, they feared the enemy's mortars. Most likely this was due to seeing their own mortar bursts from a distance appearing less impressive than artillery explosions. There was little return fire as the Japanese were cut down

A BAR man lays his gear out to dry on a shelter-half. Note the six-pocket (two 20-round magazines each) BAR belt plus the yellow-painted Mk II fragmentation grenades. The other shelter-half remains erected. Two shelter-halves buttoned together made a "pup tent," which could be erected over a foxhole. Front-line troops, though, had to leave their foxholes unprotected from the rain. (Tom Laemlein/Armor Plate Press)

in droves. The initial attack was over in ten minutes. The 1st Platoon's casualties were light. 1stSgt William McMullen, who was in the 1st Platoon area, was among the few wounded.

It was a different situation on L Company Ridge. Through the night the Japanese kept up the pressure. Falling back after their first attack, they reorganized and attacked within an hour. Again repelled with heavy losses, they harassed the ridge defenders with sporadic rifle and LMG fire. It was now daylight, but they had adequate concealment in the brush and saplings on the ridge side. The rattle-traps often alerted the Marines as the enemy crept up the limestone ridge. Being atop the ridge, Marines were exposed when they rose to fire downslope. At the point of the V-shaped ridge the Japanese laid down heavy fire, forcing a half-dozen wounded Marines to pull back 10yd below the crest. They went no farther even though Japanese occupied the crest trench. Points along the crest were taken, but the enemy was driven off by small groups of Marines counterattacking on their own without orders to do so. They otherwise had no place to go. They had no communications to the rear and they received no artillery or mortar support.

Just before noon on the 14th, Capt Spurlock ordered a 1st Platoon squad to reinforce the struggling 3rd Platoon on the ridge. 1Lt Flaherty

The Marines found that four men were necessary to carry litters owing to their being on half-rations, the rough ground, the hot and humid climate, exhaustion, lack of sleep, and – in all probability – suffering from tropical illnesses themselves. The pistol-armed litter bearer to the left carries a civilian hunting knife, a common practice. (Tom Laemlein/Armor Plate Press)

The fight at "L Company Ridge"

US view: On "L Company Ridge" 2nd and 3rd platoons of Company L, 3/5th Marines defended a shallow trench with fighting positions dug into the limestone ridge crest. Here, a rifleman with bayonet fixed moves up to the trench. The Marines had to expose their heads and shoulders to fire down the steep slope. Even then, most of the Japanese were hidden beneath the dense coconut palms below and the Marines could see little. Temporarily, grenade, mortar and artillery explosions; muzzle flashes, tracers, and flares literally blinded the ridge-top Marines. They could not even make out individual muzzle flashes to shoot at. They simply fired into where they thought the Japanese might be and ducked bullets cracking over their heads and buzzing shrapnel. The actual distribution of USMC machine guns atop the ridge is not known, but believed to be two M1917A1 water-cooled and two M1919A4 air-cooled guns (shown to the left being cleared of a jam) along with up to ten M1918A1 BARs (shown to the right). In the center a squad grenadier loads a Mk I Vivien-Bessières rifle grenade into a Mk III VB cup-type grenade launcher or "trombone" fitted on his M1903 rifle.

Japanese view: The 4th, 5th, and 6th companies of the II/124th Infantry, the Left Flank Unit, approached "L Company Ridge," what the Japanese called *Tora Oka* (Tiger Hill) under cover of darkness. Believing themselves to be farther away from the American line than they in fact were, the Japanese had not yet deployed into platoon line formations as was normal. As they emerged from the coconut palms, the Japanese were blinded by the glare of explosions and muzzle flashes. The crest of the ridge rippled with continuous muzzle flashes and red tracers streaked downslope. Here, a 7.7mm Nambu Type 99 (1939) LMG crew rushes toward *Tora Oka*, as much to flee the enemy artillery fire creeping up behind them as to assault the ridge as ordered. At this stage in the war all members of the crew were armed with 8mm Nambu Type 94 (1934) pistols, one of the worst designs used by any army in World War II, and the 15.5in Meiji Type 30 (1897) bayonet. Those Japanese making it to the ridge attempted the scramble up the steep slope through barbed wire and trip-wired grenades. None would make it to the top until daylight with renewed assaults.

personally led the squad. Avoiding a machine-gun burst on his way up the ridge, Flaherty fell backwards and was stabbed by Corp Ore J. Marion's bayonet. They commenced to argue under Japanese fire. Marion finally bandaged the officer and they made it to the crest. (Their bickering was said to go on for years at post-war reunions.) Fighting continued all day. At one point the Marines collected a half-dozen VB rifle grenades and a company mortarman appeared with a 60mm mortar tube – but no bipod – and four rounds. Hand-holding the tube with its breech end jammed into the ground, he fired the rounds almost straight up to hit the crest. Most likely the first round was a miss, but a seasoned mortarman would sense the necessary adjustments owing to his experience. The VB grenades were not impact-detonated, but had an 8-second delay fuse to allow air bursts to be achieved. Even the small VB grenade was deadly air-bursting over a trench. This sketchy firepower drove off most of the enemy. The remaining, to include the wounded, were routed out at bayonet point. After that the Americans received artillery support to blast the retreating Japanese.

The USMC squad leaders on the ridge struggled to establish a continuous defense line down to the coconut grove. Three of the four squad leaders were seriously wounded by a short US 105mm round. Reorganizing under the remaining squad leader, Corp Marion, they re-secured the crest to find only dead Japanese. There was sporadic shooting through the day and into the night, but no more Japanese attacks. Japanese stragglers made individual efforts to flee from the carnage. Some made it as the morning mist, dust, and smoke from explosions screened them from pot-shooting Marines. The next morning, September 15, the American battalion and company COs visited the ridge and organized a patrol to search the battleground. There were few dead Japanese left atop the ridge and none to be found on the forward slope and in the immediate jungle. They followed a trail of bloody dressings. Within 150yd they found a partly earth-covered pile of almost 100 dead Japanese, many killed by the previous afternoon's artillery barrages. With the area declared secure, Marines from support units appeared to search for souvenirs. Some were pressganged, much to their chagrin, into recovering and burying the Japanese dead.

The III/4th Infantry's failure to join the fight may have been a case when the commander was from a different regiment and division than the unit he was attached to and purposely failed to follow an outsider commander's orders, especially if he did not agree with the plan. This practice, known as *gekokujō*, was a rather common occurrence. Off to the south throughout the day the Americans saw Japanese stragglers from the Bloody Ridge battle, many wounded and unarmed, moving west. US patrols found bodies for days afterward, survivors of the battle who succumbed during the retreat. Oddly, a dead Japanese officer was found on L Company Ridge with two briefcases of Japanese money for which no explanation could be given.

PFC Boston commented, "We had a brave bunch of kids that night, and there were a lot of cases where medals should have been given out but were never issued, because there was no officer to see what they did, our officers being few and far between" (quoted in Marion 2004). After the battle the squads were typically down to five men each and there were now only three squads per platoon. The Kawaguchi Detachment lost almost 1,000 men on Bloody Ridge, but the flank attacks also cost the Japanese several hundred more.

The Matanikau Counteroffensive

October 23–26, 1942

BACKGROUND TO BATTLE

Following the arrival of the first US Army troops on October 13, the Americans reorganized the perimeter into five new sectors. In Sector 1, the 3rd Defense and 1st Special Weapons battalions defended 7,100yd of beach, except for the 1,000-plus yards adjacent to the west and east flanks, which were secured by the regiments defending those flanks. In Sector 2, the newly arrived 164th Infantry covered the eastern end of the beach, 6,600yd inland along the Ilu, and then west almost to Edson's Ridge. In Sector 3, Col Sims' 7th Marines (less LtCol William R. Williams' 3/7th) covered a 2,500yd front inclusive of Edson's Ridge west to the Lunga River. In Sector 4, the 3,500yd sector from the Lunga westward and curving north to include the previously unsecured area of rugged terrain was defended by the 1st Marines (less the 3/1st). In Sector 5 the 5th Marines continued to secure the important west end of the perimeter to include a portion of the beach. The perimeter here had been pushed about 1,500yd farther west, but was still 3,500yd from the Matanikau River and the main Japanese defense line. The 3/2nd Marines was the division reserve, positioned north of the airfield.

Two earlier actions had seen Marine thrusts toward the Matanikau. Both were intended as a reconnaissance-in-force and to inflict attrition upon those enemy known to be massing in the area, mainly the reinforced 4th Infantry Regiment. The first operation – First Matanikau – occurred during September 24–27 and was intended to extend the perimeter to the Matanikau to be defended by two battalions. Battalions were committed in phases. On the 24th LtCol Lewis B. "Chesty" Puller's 1/7th Marines (less detachments) swung south to the slopes of Mount Austen, worked its way to the Matanikau and turned north to the coast. The Marines engaged a Japanese force and suffered 32 casualties. The 2/5th Marines was sent to reinforce the 1/7th Marines. The next day both battalions reached the Matanikau and moved north to the river's mouth. An American attempt to force a crossing was repulsed. Traveling along the coast and tasked with establishing a patrol base at Kokumbona, 5 miles to the west, the 1st Raider Battalion reached the scene of action. Attacking the next morning, they too failed to force the river. A Japanese force had crossed the river farther south and established a blocking position on the Marine left flank. Two companies of the 1/7th Marines, A and B, were withdrawn on the 25th and conducted an amphibious landing west of the Matanikau and Point Cruz – a small knob peninsula 1,300yd west of the Matanikau River – only to be pinned down. Forced back to the beach, they were withdrawn by landing craft and took heavy losses. The Raiders and 2/5th withdrew overland. The operation failed in all its goals and resulted in the loss of almost 100 dead and over 100 wounded.

Regardless of US reinforcements, more aircraft, and an improved American supply situation, the Japanese still bombed at will, ran the Tokyo Express through almost nightly, and landed reinforcements and supplies from destroyers and barges. Four 10cm Type 92 (1932) howitzers near Kokumbona, dubbed "Pistol Petes," were out of counterbattery range and caused considerable damage on the airfields and perimeter; it was feared these, coupled with the air and naval bombardments, could combine to neutralize the airfield at inopportune times, especially when Japanese reinforcements landed or during major ground attacks. The Americans planned a six-battalion attack to swing inland, cross the Matanikau upriver – 30yd wide at this point – and turn north on three parallel routes striking along the river's west bank

The congested Beach Red near Lunga Point. The landing craft visible here include: landing craft, mechanized Mk 2 – LCM(2); landing craft, personnel (large) – LCP(L); landing craft, personnel (ramp) – LCP(R); and landing craft, vehicle, personnel (LCVP). Most of the beach within the Henderson Field perimeter was edged by palms like these. (USMC Historical Center)

and toward Point Cruz – an operation termed Second Matanikau. The goal was to push the Japanese and their artillery away from the river. As with the previous operation, it was planned to establish a stronghold at Kokumbona to keep the artillery at bay. In the meantime the Japanese had established a small bridgehead on the US-held side of the Matanikau and pulled their main line back to just beyond Point Cruz. The east bank force was a composite company of the 4th and 124th Infantry regiments. On October 7 the 3/2nd Marines and the divisional Scout-Sniper Detachment – together called the Whaling Group, after the scout-snipers' commander, Col William J. Whaling – plus the 7th Marines (less the 3/7th), moved to a ridge east of the Matanikau to bivouac. The 1st Raider Battalion moved along the coast road to attempt a river crossing the next morning. At the same time the 5th Marines (less the 1/5th) moved to a position south of the Japanese lodgment to cover the 7th Marines' morning crossing. The 3/1st Marines was the operation's reserve. The 1/11th, 2/11th, and 5/11th Marines provided artillery support.

The Japanese planned to launch an artillery-supported attack in the same area at the same time with the 4th Infantry Regiment. They had moved an enveloping force across the Matanikau on the 6th. The Whaling Group ran into them moving to its bivouac. They bypassed the Japanese and prepared for the next day's crossing. The Raiders and 5th Marines collided with the Japanese bridgehead but, although outflanking them to the south, were unable to dislodge them. On the 8th the 3/1st Marines conducted an amphibious feint just beyond Point Cruz. When taken under fire the Marines withdrew as planned. The goal was to stall the Japanese while the 5th Marines launched their attack. Rain delayed the American attack until the 9th. In the meantime, amtracs simulated tanks marshaling for an attack while the 5th Marines and Raiders chipped at the Japanese bridgehead. The Japanese attempted to break out in the evening and were largely wiped out. On the morning of the 9th, the Whaling Group and the 7th Marines crossed the upper Matanikau and swung north in three prongs. Japanese opposition was limited, but the 1/7th Marines engaged a force inland from Point Cruz, wiping it out mostly with artillery. The three US battalions returned through the 5th Marines and Raider positions on the Matanikau during mid-afternoon. Marine losses were 65 dead and 125 wounded while the Japanese lost at least 700. US intelligence indicated a larger attack was coming from the west and a new defense line was established on the Matanikau.

The 17th Army HQ had arrived on Guadalcanal on the night of October 9. Lt-Gen Hyakutake, commanding 17th Army, established his *sento shireijo* (battle command post) at Kokumbona along with concentrated artillery. Maj-Gen Sumiyoshi Tadashi, the 17th Army artillery officer, controlled 15 15cm howitzers, seven 10cm guns and howitzers, seven 7.5cm field guns, and three 7.5cm mountain guns. He would also command the Sumiyoshi Force, the infantry units attacking the Marines' Matanikau line. Naval gunfire was also to be provided. The 2nd Division's order was issued on October 10, tentatively to launch on the 18th. The Japanese goal was to regain Guadalcanal and continue with the delayed New Guinea operation. The night of the 14th saw five Japanese transports run to Tassafaronga, and in full view of the flustered Marines, debarked troops, supplies, and crew-served weapons. Barely any Marine aircraft were able to launch, although a few damaged three transports, forcing them to run aground and burn (their hulks remain in place today). Regardless, up to 4,000 troops of the 2nd Division's 16th and 230th Infantry regiments landed along with 80 percent of their supplies. There were now 20,000 Japanese on the island including those who landed earlier in October. Five transports, 27 destroyers and patrol vessels, and two seaplane carriers – for artillery – were allocated to deliver large portions of the 2nd Division (Lt-Gen Maruyama Masao) and 38th Division (Lt-Gen Sano Tadayoshi). Most of the latter would remain, for now, at Rabaul. Various Japanese artillery, engineer, medical, and support units were also landed. Some 2,000 of the 9,000-man Kawaguchi Detachment were dead and 5,000 wounded or ill.

A Marine sniper armed with an M1903 Springfield fitted with the little-used 5× Lyman 5A telescope rather than the much more common and longer 8× Unertl telescope with a larger objective lens (front end). Marine snipers were mainly employed as counter-snipers firing from front-line positions or accompanying patrols. (Tom Laemlein/Armor Plate Press)

The Japanese maintained an observation and radio post called *Mambulo* on the north side of Mount Austen to see much of the American activity. The jungle, though, prevented them from assessing Marine perimeter defenses accurately. Lt-Gen Hyakutake reset Y-Day for October 20. The Maruyama Force – the main attack in the vicinity of Edson's Ridge – would attack with the 29th Infantry Regiment as the Left Wing unit and the III/124th Infantry and 230th Infantry Regiment (less the III/230th) as the Right Wing. The 16th Infantry Regiment was the 2nd Division reserve. The supporting Japanese attack – actually a diversion for the main attack at Edson's Ridge – would be mounted by the Sumiyoshi Force, fielding three infantry battalions and a tank company and well supported by artillery. It would attack across the Matanikau toward the advanced positions of the 3/1st Marines. The Oka Force with three battalions, subordinate to the Sumiyoshi Force, would launch attacks on the exposed south flank of the Matanikau advanced positions. It is not clear why the 4th and 124th Infantry regiments exchanged their third battalions – possibly because of late arrival in the marshaling area.

The Maruyama Force departed Kokumbona on October 16–18. The march required about six days. The Marine command was unaware of this force, but expected the Matanikau attack. For the Japanese, Y-Day was moved to October 22, then the 24th. The attack was delayed yet another day, but the order was not received in time by all units. The 1st Independent Tank Company would lead the assault, crossing the sandbar at the Matanikau's mouth. It would be followed by the 4th Infantry Regiment (less the III/4th) with the III/124th Infantry in reserve – almost 2,000 troops. In the meantime Col Oka would lead the 124th Infantry Regiment (less the III/124th) and the 630-man III/4th Infantry south, cross the Matanikau over the One Log Bridge (*Nippon-bashi* – "Nippon Bridge"), and swing north to attack the Marines' left flank.

MAP KEY

1   1430hrs, October 23: Following preparatory artillery and mortar barrages during the previous day, Japanese tanks of the 1st Independent Tank Company move into assault positions and the II/4th Infantry prepares to attack; the III/124th Infantry is the follow-on force. Japanese artillery preparation continues.

2   1700hrs, October 23: The tank company advances onto the sandbar with nine tanks. The 7th Company, II/4th Infantry follows, with the 5th Company attacking on the Japanese right and the 6th Company in reserve.

3   1720hrs, October 23: All nine Japanese tanks are destroyed, including two that made it across the sandbar. The Japanese infantry is driven off by US artillery.

4   1740hrs, October 23: The 7th and 5th companies renew their attack and are halted with heavy losses.

5   2330hrs, October 23: The 6th Company attempts to wade the river 300yd upstream and is wiped out. Firing continues from both sides all night.

6   Dawn, October 24: The Japanese begin to withdraw; Marine patrols cross the river to discover 600 enemy dead.

7   Afternoon, October 24: Elements of the 3/7th Marines on Hill 67 detect elements of Oka Force (I/124th, II/24th, and III/4th Infantry) south of their position moving to attack the Americans' exposed south flank.

8   Late afternoon, October 24: The 2/7th Marines occupies the ridge to protect the south flank. Japanese forces probe the position during the night and the next day. At 2200hrs on October 25, Oka Force attacks the 2/7th Marines and loses 300 men.

Battlefield environment

During this battle the Marines found themselves in much the same tactical terrain situation as they had experienced during the battle of the Tenaru – comparatively flat terrain with sparse vegetation overlooking a shallow river "bridged" by a sandbar. The Matanikau was only about half as wide as the Tenaru, though, at 45–50yd. The sandbar was wider, however, which was of benefit to both tanks and infantry assaulting across the low sandbar. Farther upstream the river was wadeable.

The area on both sides of the Matanikau's mouth had seen a significant amount of action since September, with both sides of the river changing hands. The terrain was battle-scarred, entrenched, and cratered, with palms shattered, and littered with cast-off weapons and equipment. As in the previously described actions, the beach was narrow; the coastal road ran through the palms with more coconut plantation land beyond the road, and dense forest farther inland. On the Japanese (west) side of the river were low ridges and hills, with brush and trees on the sides and tops covered by kunai grass. The Japanese had prepared crawl trenches to allow them to occupy assault positions. These were well camouflaged by palm fronds and other vegetation debris, which littered the ground owing to the frequent shelling. The Marines were dug into spider holes and machine-gun nests with interlocking fields of fire. The two Marine battalions defending the Matanikau River line were rather exposed in that they were 3,500yd west of the main Henderson Field perimeter. The south (inland) flank of this extension was undefended except for small roving US patrols.

Much of the north-central coast, to include the area within the Henderson Field perimeter, was covered by coconut palm plantations arrayed in orderly rows. Mature trees were 30–60ft tall. Aircraft could not see what was beneath the palm tops. Between 8,000 and 10,000 natives inhabited villages scattered along the coasts and most fled to the south side during the fighting. (USMC Historical Center)

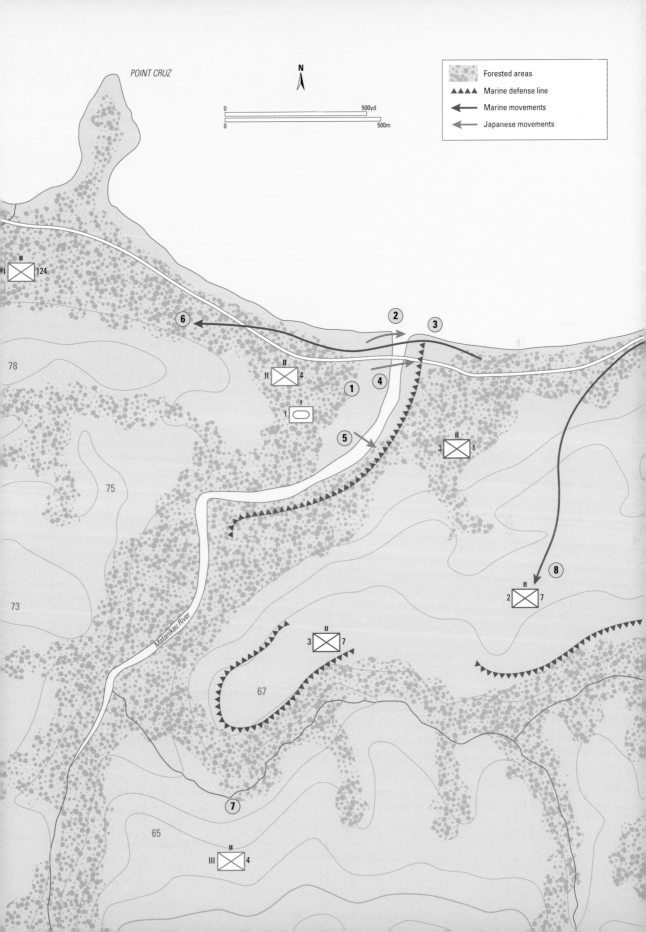

POINT CRUZ

N

Forested areas
▲▲▲▲ Marine defense line
← Marine movements
← Japanese movements

0   500yd
0   500m

II
⊠ 124

78

6

2
3

II
II ⊠ 4

1

1 ▭

4

5

II
3 ⊠ 1

75

73

Matanikau River

8

II
2 ⊠ 7

II
3 ⊠ 7

67

7

65

III II
⊠ 4

INTO COMBAT

The 7th Marines had originally served in 1917–19, 1920–22, and 1933–34. The regiment was reactivated in January 1941 by splitting the 5th Marines, and was assigned to the 1st MarDiv in Cuba. The 7th Marines was reassigned to the 3rd Marine Brigade and sent to Samoa in May 1942. As a defense force it trained in hilly jungles and a tropical environment. When deployed to Guadalcanal and reassigned to the 1st MarDiv, it was well acclimatized after four months. Arriving on September 18, the fresh troops were assigned the critical south-central Sector 3 from Edson's Ridge inclusive to the Lunga River. It would see its first action on October 7–9 during the Second Matanikau. LtCol Williams' 3/7th Marines was detached to defend Hill 67, known as *Saru* – "Monkey" – to the Japanese, overlooking the southern portion of the Matanikau Line, a 750yd concave curve in the MLR. (American hill designations were numbered in sequence and did not indicate elevation as was common practice. Hill 67 was just over 100ft above sea level and actually the west end of a higher ridge.)

The 3/1st Marines defended the northern portion of the Matanikau Line – another concave curve, 1,200yd in length – and the beach flank for about 700yd. They had used barbed wire at both ends of the sandbar, but there were no AT obstacles. Barbed wire was also strung along the west bank and booby trapped with grenades. An L-shaped sandbar crossed the river's mouth – 20–35yd wide at low tide – forcing the river to make a left angular turn. Two 37mm AT guns and two halftrack-mounted 75mm guns were dug-in to cover the sandbar. Near the mouth the bank was only a couple of feet high, what the Marines would call "Hell's Gate." It rose gradually as it progressed inland and had an average width of 45–50yd. The area around the Matanikau's mouth had been long contested, being covered by craters, blasted trees, fighting positions and trenches dug by both sides, and scattered munitions and equipment. Matanikau village on the west bank and other hut clusters had been blasted away. On both sides the rolling, hilly terrain was mostly tree- and brush-covered, but the ridge tops were grass-covered. Between the beach and forest was a narrow belt of palms with the coastal road.

The 3/1st Marines had occupied the position since after the 5th Marines cleared the east bank bridgehead on the 9th. The rest of the 1st Marines defended Sector 4 on the south-central perimeter. From right to left, the 3/1st Marines deployed its companies as follows: Company I had one platoon on the beach and two facing the river, backed by two 37mm AT guns and two dug-in halftrack-mounted 75mm guns covering the sandbar; Company K was in the center; Company L was on the left flank adjacent to the 3/7th Marines on Hill 67. An HMG platoon from Company M was attached to each rifle company. All companies' three platoons were in the line and there was no battalion reserve. They could not prepare an all-round defense, but the 3/7th Marines protected the left flank and the division reserve – the 3/2nd Marines and the 1st Light Tank Battalion – waited in readiness. The 81mm mortar platoon plotted concentrations for each company across the river along with the companies' 60mm mortars. While the 3/1st Marines was understrength – although, with 800 men, it was better off than others – it possessed its full allotment of weapons. The 1/11th and 2/11th Marines provided artillery support. Each battery plotted several 100yd-wide "strips" stretching west from the river. The

Marines were now digging deeper foxholes, allowing them to fight standing and providing better artillery protection, something they learned from the Japanese. They even called them "spider holes" as Japanese positions were called. Some sandbags were available. More barbed wire was available, enough for an apron fence and barriers on both ends of the sandbar. Rattle-traps and booby-trapped grenades dotted the wire. No AT obstacles blocked the sandbar. It appears the Marines were not aware of the landing of Japanese tanks. There were no outposts on the river's west side owing to the extent of Japanese activity. Even US patrols on the west side had ceased with the appearance of enemy tanks on October 19. This would be the first time Marines faced tanks. In spite of this, the Americans considered this to be the strongest single position yet.

A Marine sprays DDT in his "spider hole" to rid it of pests – sand fleas, spiders, scorpions, centipedes, and ants. This position has firing embrasures in the front to offer better head protection. (Tom Laemlein/Armor Plate Press)

The officer commanding the 3/1st Marines, LtCol William N. "Wild Bill" McKelvy, Jr., had a reputation of being eccentric, egotistical, hard drinking, hard on his staff, and demanding of his troops. Everyone knew it was flamboyant show to inspire the troops. He was one of two of the 12 battalion commanders in the first four regiments on the island avoiding replacement or wounds. McKelvy would tour the front line asking his men if they would retreat and offered them white minefield-marking tape to mark their escape route. All declined. As one Marine said, "After all, where the hell could you go?" (quoted in Twining 2007: 130). They knew an attack was imminent, but morale was high. Malaria, though, was thinning both sides' ranks. Marines had to have a temperature over 104°F (40°C) for hospitalization. Regardless of the ravages of malaria, leaders were having a difficult time ensuring the troops took their atabrine and quinine. Rumors claimed taking the drugs resulted in the loss of sexual prowess.

Japanese troops, other than officers, were made to stay in the line and expired on the trail or in spider holes. Things were not going well for the Japanese. Widespread illness, hunger, exhaustion, rain, flagging morale, and the inadequate trails cost time. Communications – radio, telephone, messenger – were irregular. Communication between the 17th Army and 8th Fleet was confused and not all of the constant changes and updates were being disseminated to subordinate commands on a timely basis. Owing to delays, Maj-Gen Kawaguchi was ordered relieved on the 24th, but the ill Col Shoji Toshinari of the 230th Infantry Regiment turned down the offer to take over. Kawaguchi retained command, but that could not have improved morale and confidence. The Kawaguchi Detachment ceased to exist, being absorbed into the 2nd Division.

Even though only 5 miles from Kokumbona and 17th Army HQ, the Sumiyoshi Force did not receive the date change to 1700hrs on the 24th. Instead, they would attack a day early on the 23rd. Some units were still moving into position, others in the wrong position – the attack would be launched piecemeal. The American advantage was that a battalion could be moved from one end of the perimeter to the other in three hours. For the Japanese to move a battalion from the perimeter's flank to the south-central portion around Edson's Ridge would require days and it would arrive exhausted.

Major General Alexander Archer Vandegrift, USMC

Known to friends as Archer and to his troops as "A. A." – even in person in combat – Alexander Vandegrift (1887–1973) was commissioned a 2nd lieutenant in the Marine Corps in January 1909. In 1912–23 he saw service in Cuba, Nicaragua, Vera Cruz, Mexico, and Haiti, and was greatly disappointed not to have been deployed to France with the 4th Marine Brigade during World War I. After serving in China he was promoted to brigadier general in 1940 and, after briefly serving as the 1st MarDiv's assistant commander, took command of the division on March 23, 1942 and was promoted to major general. This was unusual in that he had never commanded an infantry battalion or regiment.

Knowing he would lead the division into its first action, Vandegrift was selected for the command owing to his widely varied staff and administrative experience coupled with his military education. He quickly replaced officers failing to meet his standards. He demanded quick and decisive action from his subordinates, relieving one officer as "nothing but a damn old school teacher" (Hoffman 2001: 138). Vandegrift never forgave Admiral Frank Fletcher for withdrawing his ships,

leaving the Marines stranded without full equipment, ammunition, rations, and air support. Vandegrift's conduct of the Guadalcanal Campaign was effective, but he made mistakes. One was a late recognition of the pending Japanese attack on Edson's Ridge as he focused on defending the perimeter's flanks. He also endured a short spell of lost optimism when he thought the Japanese might overrun his division.

Vandegrift would receive the Navy Cross for the Guadalcanal/Tulagi Landing and the Medal of Honor for the difficult occupation and defense of the islands from August to December 1942. He took over command of I Marine Amphibious Corps in July 1943 and planned the Bougainville landing. After establishing the beachhead in November, he became the 18th Commandant of the Marine Corps and in April 1945 became the first active duty four-star general in the history of the Corps. He oversaw the final Marine victories in the Pacific and the Corps' post-war reduction, and fought efforts to eliminate the Corps. Vandegrift retired in April 1949; he died on May 8, 1973 and is buried at Arlington National Cemetery.

The 1st Independent Tank Company (Capt Maeda Yoshito) had moved into its assembly area during the day, one tank at a time to reduce the noise, mostly covered by surf and coastal winds. The company was organized from the 4th Company, 2nd Tank Regiment after the Netherlands East Indies Campaign. It reached Guadalcanal on October 14. Three days later, one Type 97 medium tank of 3rd Platoon was damaged by an American destroyer shelling at random. The 104-man company was organized into an HQ with one Type 97 (1937) Chi-Ha medium and two Type 95 (1935) Ha-Go light tanks, three platoons with three Type 97s, and a company train with a cargo truck and two repair vehicles. The four-man Type 97 was armed with a 5.7cm gun and the three-man Type 95 a 3.7cm. Both had two 7.7mm machine guns.

On the 19th the Japanese tank company reconnoitered the west bank, finding the only crossable point was the sandbar. The 2nd Platoon approached the riverbank without being fired on. The next day a 3rd Platoon tank was damaged by a Marine 37mm, disabling its gun. The next day the 1st Platoon knocked out a Marine AT gun. This activity alerted the Americans to the tanks' presence. No AT barriers were erected on the sandbar owing to Japanese artillery fire. Japanese artillery fired through the day, dropping the campaign's heaviest barrage yet on the 3/1st Marines, along the coastal road, and rear area installations. It was obvious that the Marine positions were on the riverbank, but much of the artillery struck in the rear. The 3/1st Marines lost six dead and 25 wounded.

The Japanese assault battalion was the II/4th Infantry under Maj Tamura Masuro. The 7th Company (Lt Ishibashi Tetsuji) would follow the tanks across the sandbar. The 5th Company (Lt Onodera Yshimi) would wade the river to the right – however, it is believed the men of this company mainly

Born on September 13, 1889 in Nagano Prefecture, northeast of Tokyo, on the main island of Honshu, Maruyama graduated from the IJA Academy in 1911 and the IJA War College in 1919. After learning English, in 1923–25 and 1934–35 he served as a military attaché in Britain, and in India during 1929–30. Between his first tour in Britain and his tour in India he served on the IJA General Staff, being responsible for US and British intelligence assessment. With his extensive experience with the British and Americans one would think that he would gain a more realistic view of their military capabilities.

After a spell on the General Staff, in 1937–38 Maruyama commanded the elite 4th Guards Infantry Regiment and saw his first action during the China Incident. In 1938 he took command of the 6th Brigade, 9th Division in China, seeing more combat, and was promoted to major-general. Promoted to lieutenant-general, Maruyama assumed command of the distinguished 2nd Division in late 1940. The division remained in Japan until January 1942 when it shipped out to French Indochina, eventually invading Java in March and securing it in nine days. The division moved to Rabaul in September after Java occupation duty and prepared to counterattack Guadalcanal. Elements began to land in September, with most of the division coming ashore in October.

Maruyama was dedicated to traditional Japanese tactics and a firm believer in outflanking and enveloping attacks as demonstrated by his strategy on Guadalcanal. His was also a strong advocate of the night attack, but he was willing to undertake the unexpected such as the catastrophic daylight attack on the Matanikau line. He equally believed in substantial artillery support. After the defeat on the Matanikau, the division was on the defensive and Maruyama fought a grueling delaying action from November to the beginning of February 1943 as the Americans pushed his starving, disease-ridden, battered force to the island's northwest end. The shattered division was evacuated to Rabaul and then to the Philippines where it was rebuilt. He gave up command of the division before it transferred to Singapore in November 1943, and retired from active duty in 1944 owing to ill-health. Maruyama died on November 11, 1957.

took the sandbar route. The 6th Company (Lt Kurnoki Junichiro) was in reserve. The 2nd Machine Gun Company (2nd Lt Sato Chikanosuke) set up its 12 Type 92 HMGs for covering fire along with two 7cm infantry guns and at least two 3.7cm AT guns.

Capt Maeda proposed the infantry would cross first with artillery and machine-gun support to clear the east bank. The tanks would be too exposed to AT fire. Instead, Sumiyoshi directed the tanks to cross first as they were protected from machine guns. They would clear the far bank of enemy machine guns, allowing the infantry to cross. The tanks and infantry would break through and head directly for the airfield 9,000yd to the east, avoiding decisive engagement. They would link up with the Maruyama Force attacking the airfield from the south after they overcame the Edson's Ridge defenders. It would be a daylight attack to achieve surprise. All previous attacks had been at night. Sgt Hara Hisakichi described the attack as "one concerted assault [to] drive the enemy to the beach and annihilate them" (quoted in Jersey 2007: 276).

At 1430hrs the Japanese tanks moved toward the sandbar and kept out of view in the forest. The infantrymen had crept forward in crawl-trenches to their assault positions. They maintained excellent noise discipline, cut wire, and removed rattle-traps and grenades. The Marines, while expecting an attack, were unaware the opposite bank was occupied by almost 1,000 enemy assault troops. The Japanese had adequate ammunition for their rifles, machine guns, and grenade dischargers. A considerable amount of artillery was available and a field hospital was set up. Because the attack was launched a day

The Japanese Type 1 (1941) backpack (*haino*) held minimal spare clothing and personal items with a blanket and shelter-half strapped to the outside. (© IWM EQU 1724)

A fully sandbagged 37mm M3A1 AT gun position. Most, though, were simply dug into open pits with low piled-sand and/or sandbag parapets. Two layers of overhead sandbags were sufficient to protect from Japanese 5cm grenade dischargers, 7cm infantry guns, and 8cm mortars. (Tom Laemlein/Armor Plate Press)

early, there would be no supporting bomber raid or naval bombardment.

When ordered to advance at 1700hrs, Capt Maeda committed all of his tanks. They attacked while it was still light so the tanks could find their way. Once the sun set an hour and a half later they would guide on the coastal road to the airfield. The Japanese were fully aware of the presence of Marine tanks, but it is not known if they realized there was a battalion with over 30 operational tanks that were more than capable of defeating Japanese tanks. As the Japanese tanks readied to advance, the II/4th Infantry's supporting weapons – HMGs, grenade dischargers, 7cm infantry guns – opened up. Marines in spider holes ducked as yellow tracers streaked over. Instead of the expected screams of *Banzai*, the Americans heard diesel engines being cranked up. The 37mm gunners ejected canister rounds and loaded AP ammunition. They knew the tanks had to cross the sandbar. They would be channelized, unable to maneuver, and would bog down in saturated sand on the sandbar's edges silhouetted against the sky and ocean. The presence of Japanese tanks was relayed back through the chain of command to Division. A USMC tank platoon was dispatched to meet them if they made it across the sandbar. 75mm halftracks of the 1st Special Weapons Battalion moved from the beach to the 5th Marines' MLR to engage the tanks if they made it past the 3/1st Marines.

Capt Maeda was certain he was charging to his death. He ordered his company to start engines, but his own tank immediately developed engine trouble. He climbed into Lt Hiroyasu Yamaji's command tank of the 3rd Platoon, which brought up the rear with only two tanks. About 500yd from the river American artillery began impacting, along with mortars. The following infantry disappeared into the forest. Realizing they were without infantry, the Japanese tankers advanced anyway with 2nd Platoon in the lead, followed by the 1st. The tanks churned onto the sandbar single file, firing their main guns. On Borneo this had caused the enemy to reveal their positions by opening fire, or had made them retreat. The American 37mm and 75mm return fire was overwhelming. In the lead, the 2nd Platoon leader's tank was hit. The other two tanks made it across the sandbar, but mired in sand and were knocked out. The 75mm AP-capped rounds penetrated the Japanese tanks' 28mm frontal armor and punched out the other side. The 1st Platoon tanks were hit or mired, then shot-up. Some tanks ran off the sandbar into the water. One of the tanks made it across the sandbar and ran

Five of the 1st Independent Tank Company's Type 97 tanks stranded on the Matanikau River sandbar. Four of Capt Maeda's tanks made it across, to be knocked out on the east side of the river. (USMC Historical Center)

over the edge of a position occupied by Pvt Joseph D.R. Champagne of Company M, 3/1st Marines. He shoved a grenade into a track. The broken track skewed it into the water where a 75mm finished it off. Champagne received the Navy Cross, the second-highest decoration for valor. Lt Hiroyasu's tank was the last to cross and was knocked out, killing Maeda and the 3rd Platoon leader. The HQ platoon's two light tanks were knocked out by artillery on the west bank. Of the 44 Japanese crewmen, only 17 survived and seven of them were wounded. The 12 tanks, delivered to Guadalcanal with so much effort, other than two dead and 11 wounded Marines, contributed absolutely nothing to the Japanese offensive. (The tanks were left on the sandbar, later blasted apart by artillery. The remains today are submerged as the sandbar receded shoreward.)

In the meantime, with the Marines focused on the tanks, the Japanese infantry were rallied and driven out of the jungle to charge across the sandbar and river. Screaming "*Banzai!*" they met rifle, machine-gun, 37mm canister, and 75mm high-explosive fire. Preplanned artillery and mortar fire rained down – 6,000 howitzer rounds in all. Japanese platoons advanced in columns, but all semblances of formations disintegrated in the dusk, smoke, blinding flashes, flares, and whining shrapnel. Sgt Haga Shohei of the II/4th Infantry described their charge: "Others in the front line, undeterred, hurtled over the dead …" (quoted in Jersey 2007: 279). Pinned down, the Japanese assault floundered. They burrowed into existing fighting positions and craters, or scraped holes in the sand.

Firing from both sides went on all night. Japanese slithered down to the river and made tree-limb bundles camouflaged with leaves in attempts to infiltrate across. Others used floating bodies. American machine-gunners and BAR-men hammered rounds into anything floating. Japanese snipers hid among the dead and fired at movement on the river's east side. Many Marines assumed snipers were in the trees and wasted ammunition. The Arisaka's long barrel ensured propellant was burnt inside the bore; this, coupled with the effective smokeless powder, made it difficult to detect muzzle flashes. Thompson bursts sounded like 6.5mm Nambu LMGs, sometimes leading Marines to believe Japanese had infiltrated across the river. Before midnight a

Death on the sandbar

As Capt Maeda's ill-fated 1st Independent Tank Company charged across the Matanikau sandbar, the men of the 7th Company, II/4th Infantry fled into the coconut palms and forest. Marine 37mm and 75mm guns immediately opened fire, knocking out five tanks on the sandbar plus two that made it across and were shot apart just yards from the sandbar. Three other tanks remaining on the west bank were destroyed by artillery. Over half the tank crews were killed or wounded, including all officers. Marine artillery and mortar fires scattered the Japanese infantry. They were soon driven out of the trees by screaming officers. The Japanese predatory artillery on the Marine positions had little effect. American casualties were light. The 7th and 5th Companies charged out of the palms and across the narrow sandbar while it was still light. 60mm and 81mm mortar and 75mm and 105mm howitzer fire fell on the scrambling Japanese infantry. Automatic weapons, 37mm canister, and 75mm HE struck them from the front. Machine guns of the 3/1st Marines burned out their barrels firing at higher rates and in longer hammering bursts than recommended. This 37mm AT gun crew is slamming out canister rounds even though most of the Japanese were beyond the 220yd range. In the foreground a rifleman precisely fires his M1903 Springfield. The Reising M50 submachine gun-armed Marine is holding its fire until the enemy closes to within 50yd. The 5th Company attempted to infiltrate across the Matanikau River throughout the night, but almost all were shot down. The 630-man II/4th Infantry ceased to exist by dawn.

small force attempted to cross the river a few hundred yards upstream from the sandbar and was wiped out. The 3/7th Marines on Hill 67 spent a relatively quiet night.

Japanese artillery continued to fire intermittently through the night and into the day. Their rate of fire was low owing to ammunition shortages, and tapered off. Before dawn the Japanese began to fall back. Marine patrols venturing across the river at dawn found hundreds of Japanese dead – at least 600 – stretching all the way back to Kokumbona. The II/4th Infantry had ceased to exist. In all the 3/1st Marines lost 25 dead and 14 wounded. During the afternoon of the 24th, the 3/7th Marines on Hill 67 detected Japanese troops 1,000yd to the south. On the hills below Mount Austen, it appeared the Japanese were attempting to envelop the two battalions on the Matanikau Line. Artillery and air strikes were called for, but the results were inconclusive. The Japanese, traveling in small units, scattered and followed different routes. They crossed the river farther upstream from the One Log Bridge. This was the Oka Force with the 124th Infantry Regiment (less the III/124th) and the III/4th Infantry. Also on the 24th, LtCol Hanneken's 2/7th Marines was pulled from the main perimeter to relieve the 3/1st Marines. The 7th Marines would take over the Matanikau Line. With the Oka Force to the south, though, the 3/1st remained in position and the 2/7th Marines moved to protect the exposed 4,000yd south flank. They dug in on a 1,400yd front behind the 3/7th Marines. This left only LtCol Puller's 1/7th Marines defending the main perimeter's entire south-central Sector 3. The 2/7th was too understrength to man so long a line, actually a series of outposts, but the Americans were dug in along a steep ridge 220–240ft above sea level. The night was relatively quiet with occasional shots and the two sides exchanged insults. The Oka Force attacked on the night of the 25th, lost 300 men, and contributed little to the 5,600-man Manuyama Force's main attack on Edson's Ridge. This occurred at 2200hrs that night and the attack was driven off by the Marines. The Japanese continued to attack the ridge on the 25th and 26th until they were utterly defeated after US reinforcements were thrown in.

That was the end of the Japanese October Offensive. It had cost them at least 3,500 dead, including a general and three regimental commanders. A US Navy/USMC report on Japanese medical conditions stated: "In the view of the closeness of the decision in some of these engagements, the narrow margin by which the capture of the airfield was adverted … it might well be that had the enemy been able to keep his forces up to strength and in good physical condition, the narrow margin of failure would have been converted to success" (quoted in Whyte 2000: 71). For the Matanikau Line attack the Japanese had essentially repeated the tactics used in the battle of the Tenaru, with the addition of tanks. Col Cates remarked, "Evidently the Japs never heard of Plutarch's [Greek biographer *c.* 46–120 AD] wise words – 'In war time it is not permitted to make the same mistake twice'" (quoted in Whyte 2000: 75). The fatal similarity was using sandbars as the main penetration point. In all fairness, Maj-Gen Sumiyoshi may not have been aware of the details of Ichiki's failed assault. MajGen Vandegrift commended LtCol McKelvy and the 3/1st Marines "for noteworthy performance of duty during the period 9 October to 1 November 1942" (quoted in Whyte 2000: 80).

After crossing the Matanikau River downstream from the mouth the day after the battle, the Marines found that resistance was light, meeting only scattered sniper fire. On the far side of the Matanikau the Marines found nothing but carnage, with at least 600 Japanese dead scattered in an area stretching from the river to beyond Point Cruz. Most were killed by artillery. Some Japanese, attempting to flee the mortar and artillery barrages, ran into the sea only to be cut down and delivered back ashore at high tide. Souvenir hunters appeared in the morning. (USMC Historical Center)

Analysis

LESSONS LEARNED: USMC

At the outset of the Guadalcanal campaign, the Marines' attitude toward the enemy was visceral. Japan had launched a deceitful sneak attack on America, damaging the fleet, defeated an army in the Philippines including a regiment of Marines, and seized Wake and Guam – both defended by Marines. There was no forgiving. America was out for revenge. Marines grew up in culture obsessed with sports. They were competitive and didn't like to lose. There was also admittedly the racial factor. The Marines were prejudiced against the "Japs" or "Nips" as they called the enemy. It was official policy to depict the Japanese as subhuman with even military publications picturing them as monkey-like and characteristically with thick eyeglasses and buckteeth. Like the Japanese, they seldom took prisoners regardless of the pleas of intelligence officers. At the same time, rumor and even official publications painted the Japanese as super soldiers, 10ft tall, proficient in jungle and night fighting, possessing extreme stamina, and able to endure incredibly harsh conditions and poor food.

As the campaign progressed the American perception of the Japanese changed drastically. It was quickly realized the Japanese would die before being taken prisoner. Beyond that, they willingly undertook suicidal attacks with little hope of surviving. They too were indifferent to taking prisoners. The Japanese reputation for deviousness increased, owing to snipers, booby-trapping their own and American dead, using wounded or feigning surrender to lure Americans into ambushes, playing dead and shooting passing troops in the back, and so on. At the same time the Japanese soldier was proved to be less than 10ft tall. Americans did not question the enemy's bravery or dedication, but came to realize that Japanese tactics and planning left much to be desired. The Marines were surprised at times and some battles were close-run affairs, but overall they found that Japanese tactics were unimaginative, simplistic, and inflexible once execution commenced. The Japanese relied on the enemy to act as they expected, and failed to react effectively if the enemy responded otherwise. While the Japanese were masters at infiltration, outflanking the enemy, and conducting effective enveloping and encircling attacks, they all too often contributed to their defeat with unimaginative and incredibly wasteful frontal attacks. The Marines also came to realize the Japanese were no better prepared for jungle warfare than they were. The Marines felt they were better trained, armed, and equipped than their opponents even if they suffered short rations, had limited ammunition, and succumbed to tropical illnesses easily. Marine tactics were rather conventional in nature, being derived from the pre-war era's European-style tactics, but they adapted quickly to Guadalcanal's climate and terrain. Marines were critical of themselves in the early weeks on the island in regards to poor sighting and camouflage of front-line and artillery positions, failure to establish enough outposts on likely approaches, sometimes overcautious reconnaissance, and poor fire discipline.

Focusing on the small-unit level, the point of the bayonet where true decisiveness was determined, changes were made for lessons learned. In April 1943 the Marines reorganized the rifle platoon, eliminating the BAR squad and instituting three 12-man rifle squads, each with two BARs. Larger squads remained combat-effective longer than nine-man squads. Bolt-action Springfields were soon replaced by semi-automatic M1s. By late 1943 the entire Fleet Marine Force was armed with M1 rifles and M1 carbines. An LMG and 60mm mortar were added to the rifle company's weapons platoon to provide three of each. The 37mm AT guns were removed from the battalion weapons company – they were incompatible with infantry foot-mobility and the tank threat was negligible in the foreseeable future. Changes in the artillery regiment saw the replacement of the 155mm howitzer battalion (transferred to corps artillery) with a second 105mm howitzer battalion, added while retaining the three 75mm howitzer battalions.

A .30-cal Browning M1917A1 water-cooled machine gun covers troops bathing off an engineer-built floating foot bridge made of 55-gallon fuel drums. As the Marines advanced they built "jeep tracks" to bring supplies forward and spanned rivers and streams with such bridges. (USMC Historical Center)

LESSONS LEARNED: IJA

The Japanese would also adjust their small-unit organization and armament, often equipping sections with two or three LMGs and a grenade discharger. Fielding of the 4.7cm Type 1 (1941) AT gun, capable of knocking out light tanks and even M4 medium tanks, was rushed and first encountered on New Georgia in mid-1943. A Japanese pamphlet from March 1943 provided an assessment of American combat methods on Guadalcanal (it can be found in full in Miller 1949: 365–68). Some of the criticism seems unjustified or may have occurred only on occasion. Also, some seems to be aimed at newly arriving Marine and Army units lacking combat experience. Other complaints seem to be based simply on the American practices being different than those of the Japanese. Also, the Japanese viewed the Americans as overly cautious while they would have charged ahead at great cost. To the Japanese, caution on the side of keeping men alive demonstrated a weakness. They were mystified why American aircraft persisted in attacking troop transports in preference to warships. It defied their logic. Another statement declared, "if we can cut off the enemy's rear areas to half the extent they do ours, their suffering will be beyond imagination" (quoted in Miller 1949: 368). Yet Japanese air and naval attacks concentrated on the airfields and ignored American logistics.

A principal Japanese complaint was the employment of American artillery. Preparatory barrages lasted up to 12 hours, beginning at dawn or at sunset the night before an attack. Being predictable, the Japanese typically began their counterbarrage at sunrise or in the afternoon when the American attack commenced. Once the Americans attacked they often halted 300–400yd before the Japanese lines, dispatched patrols, and fired more artillery and mortars. As they advanced cautiously the Americans swept the front with rifle grenades, automatic weapons, and rifles. The Japanese emphasized that if their soldiers remained in their positions, American assaults would bog down. The American halts the Japanese so belittled were actually planned phase lines. Rather than uncoordinated charges toward some distant and, realistically unobtainable, objective with some elements penetrating and others failing, the Americans kept the attack organized and their fire support coordinated. It was slow and meticulous, but reduced casualties and virtually guaranteed success. The Japanese considered this as fighting

A 1st Medical Battalion recovery ward set up in a former Japanese barracks in one of their construction camps near the airfield. Thousands of USMC personnel on Guadalcanal were hospitalized with malaria, dysentery, and other illnesses. Ill troops retained their weapons in the wards as they would be turned out to fight a Japanese breakthrough, which fortuitously was never necessary. (USMC Historical Center)

on a schedule rather than taking advantage of tactical opportunities. There were of course many times that American commanders took advantage of such opportunities when they presented themselves to exploit the situation. They were encouraged to. Americans were also criticized for avoiding night attacks while the Japanese embraced them. Not a single Japanese night attack achieved meaningful success. The Americans realized that command and control dissolved at night, there were numerous friendly-fire casualties, that fire-support coordination failed, and it was almost impossible to remain organized to establish an effective defense against counterattacks or to continue the assault.

The Japanese were impressed with American technology, especially some that did not exist. They were convinced the Americans placed microphones forward of their lines that alerted them of Japanese advances. They admitted they never discovered the microphones, but did detect the wires. The reality was that the wires were for telephones used by outposts. American outposts either covertly withdrew to warn their unit or telephoned a warning and remained hidden. Japanese outposts and sentries typically engaged advancing Americans to slow them and warn their unit by gunfire. The so called Japanese "snipers" were simply lone sentries – which the Japanese distributed more densely than American outposts – sacrificing themselves with warning shots. Some believed the Americans used remote-controlled machine guns, possibly because when gunners were knocked out, other Marines took over. While Japanese soldiers were taught to operate LMGs, often when the gunner and Number 2 were killed, others failed to take up the gun as no one ordered them to do so. They also thought that the Americans possessed "automatic artillery" owing to the rapid and prolonged rate of fire they achieved.

Besides being impressed with the amount and speed of American artillery, there were other tactical aspects the Japanese admired. They noted that American units tied in their flanks with adjacent units and protected their rear, making outflanking and infiltration difficult. They were envious of the amount of ammunition and supplies, especially of what they considered luxury items. Even in the first three months, when the Marines were logistics-poor, the Japanese felt the enemy were better supplied than themselves. The Japanese also found engineer construction capabilities impressive, describing American airfields and communications networks as "beautiful things" (quoted in Miller 1949: 368).

The Japanese did admit that American offensive tactics improved with experience and that it was a mistake to think their tactics or doctrine were fixed. The Japanese believed in a single, decisive, winner-take-all battle – emulating the 1905 battle of Tsushima, when a small Japanese fleet utterly defeated a much larger Russian fleet during the Russo-Japanese War. The Americans would establish a solid position in strength, build up logistics, and attack with artillery and air support. The Japanese never understood why the Americans gradually penetrated into positions, extended their flanks, and pushed deeper rather than breaking into the depth of their position in one decisive blow. Yet no Japanese attempt to penetrate American positions in one all-out attack ever succeeded. In the end, the Japanese belief that their battle spirit and superior will would defeat less-resolute enemies was proven to be unfounded.

Aftermath

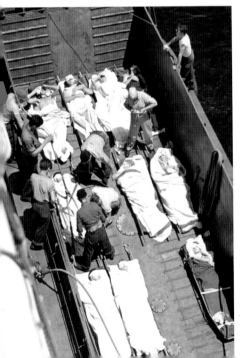

Wounded Marines are transferred from an LCM(2) to a troop transport. All of these men have head wounds, which were common as the head was exposed when firing from foxholes. Both canvas and wood litters and metal Stokes basket litters are used. C-47 transports also evacuated critical casualties from Guadalcanal. (USMC Historical Center)

The Guadalcanal Campaign dragged on for six grueling months from August 7, 1942 to February 9, 1943. The 1st and 2nd MarDivs and the Army's Americal and 25th Infantry divisions – 60,000 troops altogether – would fight there against the 2nd and 38th divisions and the 35th Infantry Brigade plus elements detached from other Japanese divisions. At the beginning of November the Marines, reinforced by additional Army units, began to push westward from the Matanikau Line. The eastern side of the perimeter was cleared, all the way to Koli Point. The tempo picked up in December. At one point so many American units were exhausted that the Composite Army-Marine Division (CAM Div) was formed by those Marine and Army

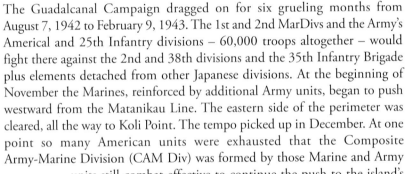

units still combat-effective to continue the push to the island's northwest end. The Japanese were able to evacuate 13,000 troops from Cape Esperance by destroyers on the nights of February 1/2, 4/5, and 7/8, 1943, in Operation *Ke*. The Empire of Japan had experienced its first defeat by a foreign army since 1598.

In all, 33,600 17th Army and 3,100 SNLF personnel fought on the island. Over 14,800 died, 8,500 in action, and 1,000 were taken prisoner. Thousands died of disease and starvation. Marine casualties ashore were 1,097 dead, 109 died of wounds, 2,916 wounded, and 298 missing and presumed dead. The US Army lost over 600 dead and missing and more than 1,400 wounded. Thousands of Marines and soldiers were disabled, at least temporarily, by illness, injury, exhaustion, and battle fatigue. Many of the Marine unit commanders and staff officers were older officers and while possessing Banana War and China experience, many were unable to endure the environmental hardships and mental strain. Younger officers would henceforth assume leadership roles.

It would not be until the end of December 1943 that the 1st MarDiv was rested, rebuilt, and retrained in Australia to conduct the Cape Gloucester Landing on New Britain. It would later endure bitter actions on Peleliu in December 1944 and Okinawa in April 1945. From September 1945 to June 1947 it occupied North China. The 2nd MarDiv executed its next operation, Tarawa, in November 1943 after rebuilding in New Zealand. The division next assaulted Saipan in May 1944 and Tinian in July. While held in reserve for Okinawa, its 8th Marines fought ashore. The 2nd MarDiv conducted occupation duty in Japan until July 1946. Many of the wounded and otherwise unfit Marines of the 1st and 2nd MarDivs were returned to the States and were invaluable passing on their skills in training assignments. Other 1st MarDiv Guadalcanal veterans remained in the division for New Britain and some even for Peleliu. Numerous 2nd MarDiv Guadalcanal veterans fought on Peleliu, but most had rotated to the States by the time of the Saipan operations.

The Japanese 2nd Division was combat ineffective when evacuated to the Shortlands. It was subsequently rebuilt in the Philippines and sent to Singapore and then to Burma. It was virtually wiped out by the British and the remnants moved to Indochina in early 1945 where it was disbanded at the war's end. Only parts of the 38th Division fought on Guadalcanal. Other elements were subsequently wiped out on New Guinea, New Georgia, and the Admiralties. The division was partly rebuilt at Rabaul where it sat out the war. Many of the surviving Japanese Guadalcanal veterans were unfit for combat duty, but were retained in infantry units regardless. Those who were unquestionably unfit for combat were often placed in security, labor, line-of-communications, and other occupation units.

In effect, a line was drawn. The Japanese would thrust no farther south to endanger the Southern Lifeline linking Australia and New Zealand with the United States. During this same period, the Australians were pushing back the Japanese on the Kokoda Trail in Papua. The fight for Guadalcanal foreshadowed what was to come over the next 30 agonizing months. When Allied forces assaulted a Japanese-held island, in spite of what the defenders and their outside support undertook, the Japanese would be utterly defeated.

The Japanese transport *Yamazuki Maru*, grounded on November 15, 1942. Alongside it rests one of the three Type A mini-submarines deployed to Guadalcanal and launched from mother submarines off the north end of the island. *Ha-11* attacked the miscellaneous auxiliary (cargo ship) USS *Majaba* (AG-43) damaging it with one of two torpedoes. *Ha-11* was scuttled for unknown reasons and its two-man crew swam ashore. (Tom Laemlein/Armor Plate Press)

ORDERS OF BATTLE

Battle of the Tenaru, August 19–21, 1942

USMC defenses at the Ilu River
HQ, 1st Marines

2nd Battalion, 1st Marines (south portion of the Ilu River Line): Companies E–H; Detachments, Battery B, 1st Special Weapons Battalion; Company C, 1st Engineer Battalion

1st Battalion, 1st Marines (initially division reserve, then north portion of Ilu River Line): Companies A–D

2nd, 3rd, and 5th Battalions, 11th Marines (fire support)

Platoon, Company A, 1st Light Tank Battalion

1st Echelon, Ichiki Detachment
HQ, Ichiki Detachment

II Battalion, 28th Infantry Regiment: 1st–4th Rifle Companies; 2nd Machine Gun Company; Platoon, Infantry Gun Unit

1st Company, 7th Engineer Regiment

Henderson Field Attack, September 12–14, 1942

USMC west flank defenses
3rd Battalion, 5th Marines: Company I, K–M

1st Battalion, 11th Marines (fire support)

IJA Left Flank Unit
II Battalion, 124th Infantry Regiment (main attack): 5th–7th Rifle companies; 2nd Machine Gun Company

III Battalion, 4th Infantry Regiment (reserve): 9th–12th Rifle companies; 3rd Machine Gun Company

Matanikau Counteroffensive, October 23–24, 1942

USMC Matanikau river line defenses
HQ, 7th Marines

1st Battalion, 7th Marines (north portion of Matanikau River Line): Companies A–D; Detachment, 1st Special Weapons Battalion

3rd Battalion, 7th Marines (south portion of Matanikau River Line – Hill 67): Company I, K–M

3rd Battalion, 2nd Marines (division reserve): Company I, K–M

1st, 2nd, and 5th battalions, 11th Marines (fire support)

Sumiyoshi Force
1st Independent Tank Company

4th Infantry Regiment (less III Battalion): Regimental HQ; I Battalion; II Battalion; Antitank Company; Regimental Gun Company

III Battalion, 124th Infantry Regiment (reserve)

In the jungle, even with vegetation blasted partly clear by artillery, visibility was limited to a few yards. Often a man could only see the man on either side of him and at night he may well have been alone and would become separated if he released his grip on pack of the man in front of him. (Tom Laemlein/Armor Plate Press)

BIBLIOGRAPHY

Bergerud, Eric M. (1996). *Touched by Fire: The Land War in the South Pacific*. New York, NY: Penguin.

Cameron, Craig M. (1994). *American Samurai: Myth, Imagination, and the Conduct of Battle in the First Marine Division, 1941–1951*. New York, NY: Cambridge University Press.

Daugherty, Leo J. III (2002).. *Fighting Techniques of a Japanese Infantryman, 1941–45*. St. Paul, MN: MBI Publishing, 2002.

Daugherty, Leo J. III (2000). *Fighting Techniques of a US Marine, 1941–45*. St. Paul, MN: MBI Publishing.

Frank, Richard B. (1992). *Guadalcanal: The Definitive Account of the Landmark Battle*. Harmondsworth: Penguin.

Hammel, Eric M. (1992). *Guadalcanal: Starvation Island*. Pacifica, CA: Pacifica Press.

Hixon, Carl K. (1999). *Guadalcanal: An American Story*. Annapolis, MD: Naval Institute Press.

Hoffman, Jon T. (2001). *Chesty: The Story of Lieutenant General Lewis B. Puller, USMC*. New York, NY: Random House.

Hough, LtCol Frank O.; Ludwig, Maj Verle E.; & Shaw, Henry I. Jr. (1958). *History of US Marine Corps Operations in World War II: Pearl Harbor to Guadalcanal, Vol. I*. Washington, DC: US Government Printing Office. Available online at http://www.ibiblio.org/hyperwar/USMC/I/index.html (accessed April 3, 2014).

Hoyt, Edwin P. (1982). *Guadalcanal*. New York, NY: Stein & Day.

Inui, Genjirou (1992). *My Guadalcanal*. Available online at http://www.nettally.com/jrube/genjirou/genjirou.htm (accessed April 3, 2014).

Ienaga, Saburo (1978). *The Pacific War*. New York, NY: Pantheon Books.

Jersey, Stanley C. (2007). *Hell's Islands: The Untold Story of Guadalcanal*. College Station, TX: Texas A&M University Press.

Leckie, Robert (1999). *Challenge for the Pacific: The Bloody Six-month Battle for Guadalcanal*. Cambridge, MA: Da Capo Press.

Manchester, William (1980). *Goodbye, Darkness: A Memoir of the Pacific War*. New York, NY: Little, Brown & Co.

Marion, Ore J. (2004). *On the Canal: The Marines of L-3-5 on Guadalcanal, 1942*. Mechanicsburg, PA: Stackpole.

Miller, John, Jr. (1949). *Guadalcanal: The First Offensive*. Washington, DC: Center of Military History. Available online at http://www.history.army.mil/books/wwii/GuadC/GC-fm.htm (accessed April 3, 2014).

Paull, William T. (1996). *From Butte to Iwo Jima: The Memoirs of William Paull*. Available online at http://www.sihope.com/~tipi/marine.html (accessed April 3, 2014).

Rottman, Gordon L. (2001a). *US Marine Corps Order of Battle: Ground and Air Units in the Pacific War, 1939–1945*. Westport, CT: Greenwood.

Rottman, Gordon L. (2001b). *World War II Pacific Island Guide: A Geo-Military Study*. Westport, CT: Greenwood.

Tregaskis, Richard W. (1943). *Guadalcanal Diary*. New York, NY: Random House.

Twining, Merrill B. (2007). *No Bended Knee: The Battle for Guadalcanal*. Novato, CA: Presidio Press.

Whyte, William H. (2000). *A Time of War: Remembering Guadalcanal, A Battle without Maps*. New York, NY: Fordham University Press.

INDEX

Figures in **bold** refer to illustrations.